Easy-going
SEWING

67250

Editor: Mary Harding
Assistant Editor: Margo Coughtrie
Editorial Assistants: Sally Fisher, Kitsa Caswell
Consultants: Patsy North, Greta Barrett
Design Coordinator: Jan Churcher
Production Control: Sheila Biddlecombe
Editorial Director: Graham Donaldson

INTRODUCTION

This book has what every woman needs — a practical collection of patterns for your home, yourself, and your family. The emphasis is on simplicity and, as long as you can stitch a seam, you will be able to make any of the items illustrated with the greatest of ease. Many of them can be completed in an evening or two, so you can see the results of your efforts in no time at all.

Sewing your own cushions, curtains, and bedcovers is a wonderful way of creating a unique home environment at the minimum cost, especially if you use remnants of bright fabrics in clever ways. *Easy-Going Sewing* gives you a colorful selection of home ideas, many of which would make lovely presents, too.

Our dressmaking patterns are also designed with practical simplicity and cost in mind. There are skirts, dresses, beach wear, nightdresses, and aprons for your own wardrobe, plus a collection of charming outfits for babies, toddlers, and older children. The uncomplicated designs allow you to take full advantage of the exciting range of fabrics available today.

Easy-Going Sewing proves that simple designs do not mean boring ones. They mean designs that are fun to make, with the minimum effort and the maximum impact.

ISBN 0 7026 0026 1

CONTENTS

Easy to make from bright triangles
Sunscreen

You and your children will
find many uses for the
tents and screens
you can make from
these triangles.

Sunscreen or windscreen: Make this protective awning from two small and three large tent poles and six triangles.

Long tent: Make this from two tent poles and eight triangles. Ideal for beach or garden, it's big enough for all the family.

1 <u>Materials Required</u>: Canvas, sail-cloth, or tarpaulin: 140 cm (55″) wide, 3 m (3¼ yds) for 3 triangles. Eyelet tool. Eyelets: 10 mm (³⁄₈″) in diameter, 21 pairs per triangle. Heavy-duty thread. Nylon cord. Thick towelling to make 5 cm (2″) toggles for each pair of eyelets.

2 Draw the triangles on the fabric with a ruler and tailor's chalk. Each side should measure 150 cm (59″) in length.

3 Turn under the edges 2 cm (³⁄₄″) on all three sides, pinching them back firmly or pressing them down. Stitch with a thick needle and strong thread in zigzag stitch.

4 Mark and punch the holes for the corners. Then mark and punch the holes along the sides, regularly spaced

about 21 cm (8¼″) apart. Place a board under the fabric to protect the working surface.

5 Insert the eyelets: Place the cap in the groove of the punch and draw the fabric over.

6 Place the eyelet ring onto the shaft and the top part of the tool on top; hammer together.

7 Join the triangles with short toggles made from dowelling and nylon cord. Drill a hole through the center of each toggle.

8 This last photograph shows the cutting layout. 3 m (3¼ yds) of fabric will give you three triangles with 2 cm (³⁄₄″) seam allowances. The half triangles can be seamed up the middle for a fourth triangle.

Square tent: Use one tent pole and four triangles for this play tent. It's easy enough for the children to put up themselves.

3

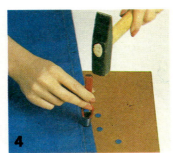
4

5

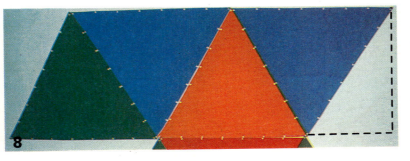
8

Making the triangles

The triangle is a basic shape which can be used to create tents, awnings, and screens of various shapes and sizes. We made triangles of brightly-colored plain canvas with equal sides and used them to make a number of clever designs to prove their versatility. There are many fabrics available for making up tents and awnings, of which canvas, sailcloth, and tarpaulin are just a few. They come in many weights, widths, and colors, too, so your choice should be guided by the requirements of your design. Look around in large stores, shops that specialize in heavyweight fabrics, and ship's chandlers.

The triangles illustrated were made up in medium-weight fabric 140 cm (55") wide. Always choose a thread suitable for the weight and fiber of the fabric being used.

Follow the step-by-step photographs for making up and joining the triangles. The eyelets are inserted with a special tool or punch. For every triangle you will need 21 eyelets and a punch with a diameter of approximately 10 mm ($\frac{3}{8}$"). Join the triangles together with toggles made from dowelling and nylon cord. Drill holes in the center of the dowels, thread the cord through, and knot the ends together. Thread the loop through the two eyelets and slip the dowel through the loop. Experiment with the length of the cord so that the pieces are joined closely as shown in picture 7. To put up the tent, screen, or awning, you will also require tent poles, tent pegs, and guy ropes. These are all available from specialist shops and camping departments of stores.

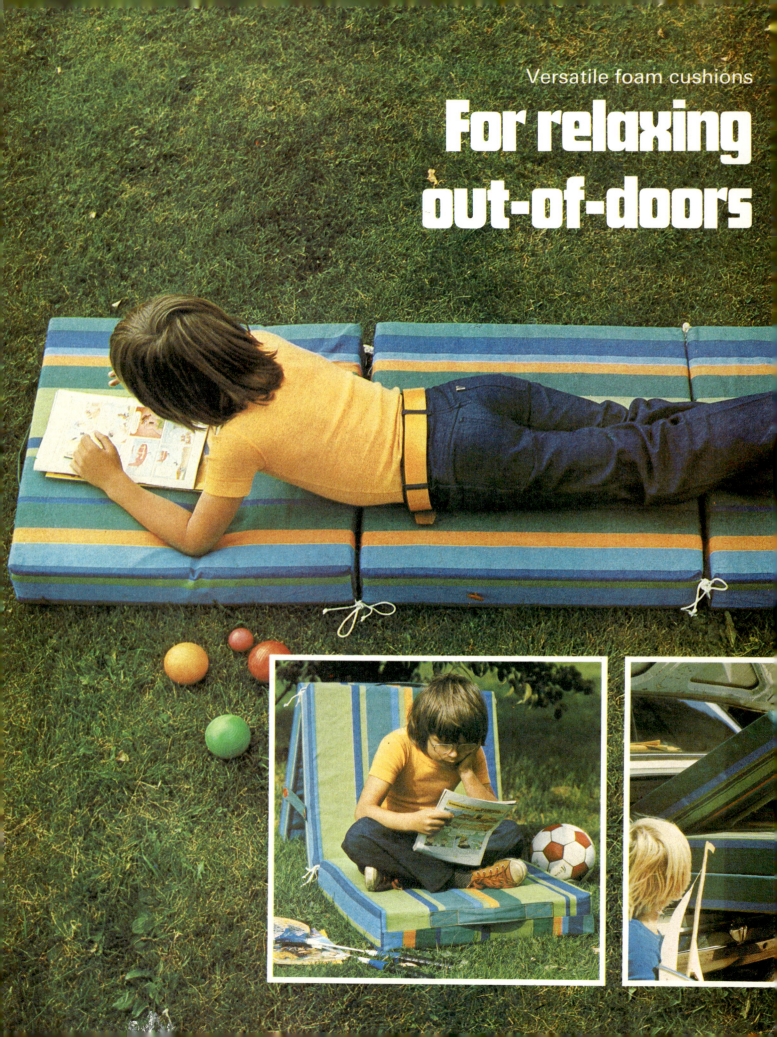

For relaxing out-of-doors

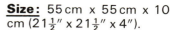

▲ Nylon cords join the cushions into a mattress. Catch the ties in at the corners so that the cushions lie flat against one another when packed away.

◀ Two of the cushions have handles which are stitched on off-center so that they lie close together for carrying purposes.

If you wish to prop up the cushions as a chair, connect the back 2 sections with a strip of fabric and 2 buttons at either side to hold them firm.
▼

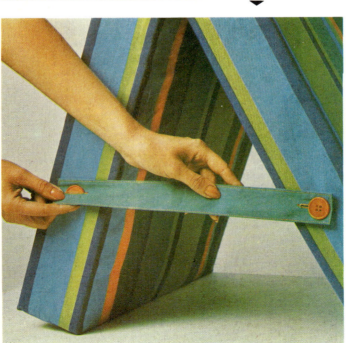

Size: 55 cm x 55 cm x 10 cm (21½″ x 21½″ x 4″).

Materials Required: Canvas: 2.10 m (2¼ yds), 140 cm (54″) wide *or* 4 m (4⅜ yds), 90 cm (36″) wide. Buttonhole thread. 3 foam rubber pads: 55 cm x 55 cm x 10 cm (21½″ x 21½″ x 4″). Nylon cord: 2.40 m (2⅝ yds). Heavyweight sewing machine needle. 4 buttons.

Cutting out: Cut out each cover, plus 1 cm (⅜″) seam allowance all around. For handles and connecting strips: Cut 2 strips for each, measuring 7 cm (2¾″) wide by 32 cm (12½″) and 45 cm (17¾″) long respectively plus seam allowance. Cut 8 cords, each 30 cm (11¾″).

Sewing: Join the seams as follows: First stitch along **a–b**, then **c–d**, including the seam allowance at either end. At the remaining open side, stitch 6 cm (2½″) at each end. Stitch corners, catching in cords (see photograph). For handles, turn in seam allowance, fold lengthwise, top-stitch all around. Stitch to sides with a decorative cross. Insert cushions; slip-stitch openings. Make connecting strips as for handles, plus buttonholes. Add buttons.

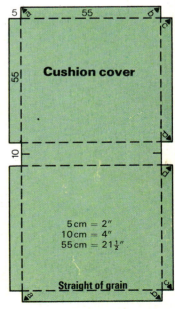

Cushion cover

5 cm = 2″
10 cm = 4″
55 cm = 21½″

Straight of grain

Cut out the cushions according to measurements on the diagram.

Cushion comfort

If you have any garden chairs made of cane or wood, you will need cushions to make them really comfortable. We show you here three different types of cushion which you can adapt to the shape of your chairs by drawing paper patterns of the seat and back. Make them in a strong fabric such as sailcloth.

Chairs 1 and 2: Straight-sided cushions made of 6 cm (2½″) thick foam rubber blocks.

Chairs 3 and 4: Shaped cushions filled with foam chips held in place with covered buttons.

Chair 5: Padded cover stitched in sections and stuffed with cushions.

If the chair is a reclining one add two or three more sections for extra length, or a removable extension with an open-ended zipper.

Cushions with straight edges

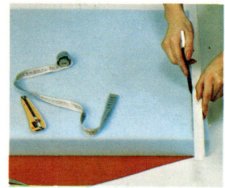

Mark the measurements of the chair seat onto the foam rubber block with a felt-tipped pen and ruler. Any curves should be marked with the help of a paper pattern which you have previously prepared.

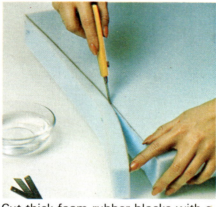

Cut thick foam rubber blocks with a sharp craft knife, holding the blade exactly perpendicular and straight. Thinner sheets of foam rubber (up to 3 cm (1") thick) can also be cut with scissors which have been wetted.

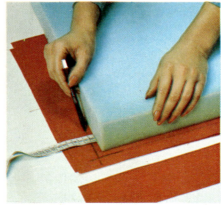

Mark the top and bottom of the cover with a 1 cm ($\frac{3}{8}$") seam allowance and cut out. Cut out 3 side

strips to fit the thickness of the foam rubber plus 1 cm ($\frac{3}{8}$") seam allowance. Divide the back strip in two (for zipper); cut out with seam allowance. Stitch in zipper.

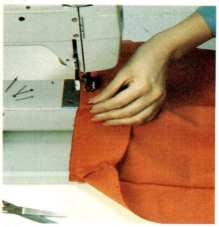

Join the 4 gusset pieces into a circle and stitch to both top and bottom, right sides facing. Leave the zipper open and turn to right side.

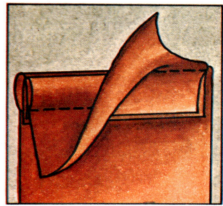

Make a second seam in the same way as a French seam all around the top and bottom, stitching close to the edges as shown. This makes the straight edges crisp.

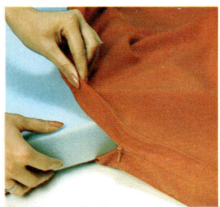

Push the foam rubber block into the fabric cover, fitting the edges along the seams.

13

Shaped cushions with buttons

Materials Required: Foam rubber chips, sheets of foam rubber 1 cm ($\frac{3}{8}$") thick. Spray adhesive. Covering fabric. Upholstery buttons.

Make a pattern for the chair seat and draw around it onto the sheet of foam rubber. Cut out with scissors.
It is advisable to wet the scissors in between cuts.

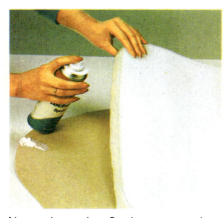

Now place the 2 sheets together and spray the cut edges all around with adhesive. Leave an opening of about 15 cm–20 cm (6"–8") on one side for filling with the foam rubber chips.

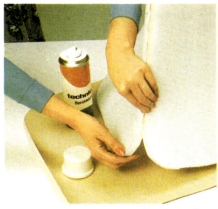

Leave the adhesive to dry for a few minutes before proceeding. The adhesive-covered edges of the foam sheets must now be placed exactly onto one another and pressed together firmly.

Now stuff the foam cushion with the foam chips, but do not fill it too full.
The opening is then glued together in the same way as the other edges.

Cut out the cover from the fabric, using a paper pattern for the seat or the foam cushion as a guide. Add 1 cm ($\frac{3}{8}$") all around for seam allowance. Stitch the cover together, right sides facing and leaving a 20 cm (8") opening. Snip into the seam allowance at frequent intervals all around.

Insert a zipper if desired. Place the cushion into the cover. If you do not require a zipper, join the opening by hand. Sew on the covered buttons with doubled buttonhole thread, sewing through all thicknesses.

Padded cover

Cut out 2 pieces of fabric to the required size. Join along 1 long and 2 short sides, turn, and stitch across at about 20 cm (8") intervals, stopping 1 cm ($\frac{3}{8}$") from the edge of the open long side.

To stuff the sections, make small cushions: stitch 3 sides together, turn, and fill with foam chips. Sew the last seam from the right side.

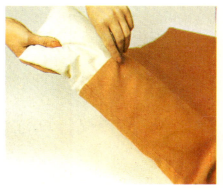

Push the foam-filled cushions into the sections of the cover. Turn in the seam allowance along the open side and stitch close to the edge. Finally, top-stitch the other 3 sides close to the edge, taking care not to catch in the cushions.

Padded towelling beach mat
Sunspot

Relax in comfort on our wonderfully soft beach mat. We have made it striped on one side, plain on the other, but you can, of course, use the same fabric on both sides. It rolls up easily into a very small space and it can be washed in the washing machine.

Size: The finished beach mat is 85 cm (33½″) wide and 180 cm (70″) long.

Materials Required:
Striped towelling: 1.85 m (2 yds), 90 cm (36″) wide. Plain towelling: 1.85 m (2 yds), 90 cm (36″) wide. Machine-washable batting or wadding: 1.80 m (2 yds), 90 cm (36″) wide.

Making the mat
Cut the batting or wadding to measure the size of the mat without the seam allowance [i.e. 85 cm (33½″) x 180 cm (70″)]. Baste onto the wrong side of the plain fabric, leaving a 2.5 cm (1″) border all around. Divide the mat into 4 equal parts lengthwise; mark divisions with basting thread. Stitch the divisions. Stitch the striped fabric to the plain fabric, right sides facing, with a 2.5 cm (1″) seam allowance, leaving about 30 cm (11¾″) open on one short side for turning. Turn through to the right side and sew up the opening by hand.

Now divide the mat into 10 sections widthwise with basting thread. Stitch along the marked divisions. The plain side is thus divided up into squares, whereas the striped side has only widthwise seams. In this way, the batting or wadding is held firmly and will not bunch up.

Playtime cushions

Pile on the cushions!

Give a trio of lively youngsters a heap of giant cushions, a lot of room and a few hours to play and they'll have the time of their lives.

What games you can invent with cushions almost your own size! You can use them for pillow fights, for a trampoline, as cuddly toys, for building a cosy nest, a dark cave, or a fortress.

Size: 75 cm (29$\frac{1}{2}$") square.
Materials Required: For each cushion: Unbleached cotton for inner cover: 80 cm x 160 cm (31$\frac{1}{2}$" x 63"). Foam chips or kapok: 2.5 kg (5 lbs.). Cotton cover fabric: 80 cm x 160 cm (31$\frac{1}{2}$" x 63").
Cutting out: Cut 2 pieces of unbleached cotton 76 cm (30") square plus 1 cm ($\frac{3}{8}$") seam allowance all around. Cut 2 pieces of cover cotton 75 cm (29$\frac{1}{2}$") square plus 1 cm ($\frac{3}{8}$") seam allowance all around.
Sewing: Stitch unbleached cotton pieces together, leaving an opening for stuffing. Turn, stuff, and sew up opening by hand. Place cover pieces together, right sides facing and stitch three sides and 2 cm ($\frac{3}{4}$") in from each corner on fourth side. Turn to right side, insert cushion, sew the opening closed.

17

A cosy corner for little girls

Our giant cushions are not only ideal for romping games, but they also make marvellous improvised furniture for children.

Cover all the cushions with the same fabric and sew on lengths of tape at intervals around the edge. The cushions

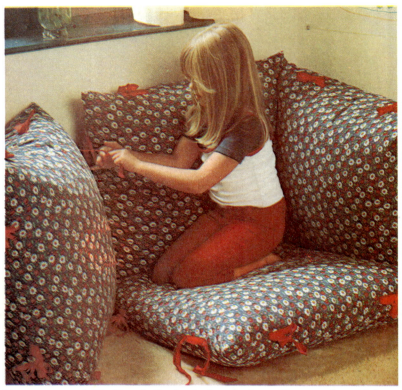

It's so easy to build this soft 'furniture'. Just tie the cushions together with bows.

By tying four of the giant cushions together, you can make a lovely, soft easy chair.

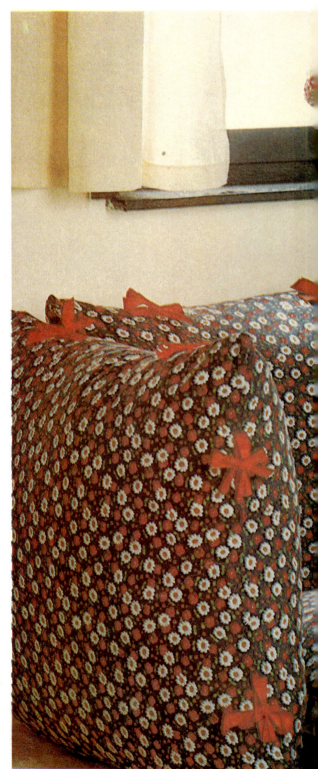

can then be tied together to form an easy chair or a cosy two-seater sofa. They will even double as a small bed for a young overnight guest.

This 'furniture' is not quite sturdy or steady enough to stand up on its own. The cushions must be leaned against a rigid support such as a cupboard or the wall. They will be even firmer if the tapes are tied into knots instead of bows. The tapes which are not in use can be tied into neat bows all round the edge to keep them from looking untidy.

Six cushions build a cosy little sofa which can double as a bed for young guests.

Cushions to make in an hour

The giant nursery cushions shown on the previous pages are very quick and simple to make. Be sure to check that the cotton cover fabric is pre-shrunk before sewing it together.

1 Materials required to make one cushion: Unbleached cotton for inner cover 80 cm x 160 cm (31½″ x 63″). Foam chips: 2.5 kg (5 lb). Cotton cover fabric 80 cm x 160 cm (31½″ x 63″). One 70 cm (28″) zipper. The size of the finished cushion is 75 cm (29½″) square.

2 Cut out two pieces of cotton measuring 76 cm (30″) square, plus a 1 cm (⅜″) seam allowance all around. Stitch the edges together all around, leaving an opening of about 25 cm (10″) on one side for the stuffing. Turn, then stuff the cushion and sew up the opening by hand.

3 Cut two pieces of cover fabric 75 cm (29½″) square, plus 1 cm (⅜″) seam allowance. Stitch around three sides and 2 cm (¾″) in from the corners on the fourth side. Turn the cover to the right side; pin and stitch the zipper in place. Or, as an alternative slip-stitch the opening closed.

4 To tie the cushions together, use firm cotton tape in a matching or contrasting color. For one cushion, you will need 4.80 m (5¼ yds) of tape. Cut it into 8 pieces, each measuring 60 cm (24″) long and trim the raw ends neatly. Each tape is stitched down twice: the first time 15 cm (6″) from the corner of the cushion, the second time 9 cm (3½″) further on. The loose ends of tape are therefore 25.5 cm (10¼″) long. Sew on the tape with heavy-duty thread or button thread for strength, catching in the inner cover to secure it because the tapes will be under quite a lot of strain when tied together.

Kitchen
curtains in

Barber pole stripes

The finished size of *each* curtain of the pair should be the same as the height by the width of the area to be covered (this allows for fullness when the curtain is closed). Make a diagram of the two curtain halves, side by side, so the stripes will be continuous when the curtains are pulled across the window. Enlarge the diagram to actual size and make tissue paper pattern pieces, adding 1 cm ($\frac{3}{8}$″) seam allowance, 2 cm ($\frac{3}{4}$″) for sides and top, and 4 cm (1$\frac{1}{2}$″) for hem at bottom. To determine the amount of fabric required for each color, arrange strips side by side and end to end to work out the most economical width and length of fabric to use. Pin pieces along the lengthwise threads of the fabric and cut out the strips. With right sides together, pin and stitch the strips. Finish all raw seam allowance edges with zigzag stitch. Press seam allowances toward the darker color. .

Turn in allowance at side edges, turn under raw edge, and stitch in place. Caution! The fabric is cut on the bias along the outside edges, so don't stretch the fabric when stitching. Turn in allowances at top and bottom as for sides and stitch in place. If you wish to gather the curtains along the top, cut two pieces of elastic or bias tape which measure a little more than half the width of each curtain half. Pull one piece through the casing formed at the top of each curtain half and stitch to curtain half at each end. Arrange gathers evenly and sew on curtain rings.

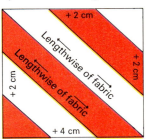

Plan the curtains carefully before beginning. Draw diagrams of the curtains side by side so the stripes will be continuous when the curtains are closed.

Curtain creations with simple trims

For the prettiest, most economical curtains in your home, just take a look at the ideas given here and choose the one that best suits your room and style of furnishings. All our curtains are made of muslin (Am) or calico (Eng). Each curtain in our pairs is 235 cm (92") long by 150 cm (59") wide, but of course your curtains will have to fit the height and width of your own windows. Before making the curtains, it is advisable to wash the fabric to avoid shrinkage later. Washing will also soften the fabric. Before trimming the curtains, turn under the hem 4 cm ($1\frac{5}{8}$"), the side seams 1 cm ($\frac{3}{8}$"), and the upper edge 2 cm ($\frac{3}{4}$"). Make valances in double fabric as they hang straight and must therefore be stiffer.

Ruffled curtains

On these curtains, the bottom corners of the inner edges are rounded off in a large curve. Press under 2 cm ($\frac{3}{4}$") all along the curve. For the ruffle, cut a straight strip 15 cm (6") wide. For the length, measure the curtain edge and add half again. Press the strip in half lengthwise and finish the edges together with zigzag stitching. Gather the strip to the required length and pin this edge of the ruffle 0.5 cm ($\frac{3}{16}$") under the pressed edge of the curtain. Place the remaining seam allowance of curtain over the edge of the ruffle, turn it in, and stitch close to the edge through all layers of fabric from the right side. The loops holding back the curtains are worked as for the ruffles, with fabric strips stitched over the edges.

Curtains with hearts

These curtains look especially pretty in a nursery or teenage girl's bedroom. Heart shapes of equal size are cut from various cotton prints and appliquéd to the curtain — a good way to use up scraps of fabric. Our heart pattern fits inside a 10 cm (4") square. Cut out the hearts and either pin them to the fabric or iron them on with bonding net. Then stitch them on with a close zigzag stitch in a matching thread. They are positioned in staggered rows 40 cm ($15\frac{3}{4}$") apart vertically and 20 cm (8") apart horizontally (measured from the center of the heart).

Curtains with lace insertion

The insertion is stitched in 12 cm ($4\frac{3}{4}''$) from the inner side and hem edges, and 7 cm ($2\frac{3}{4}''$) from valance edge. First measure the hem and side length of the insertion, then miter the corner as follows: Fold the insertion widthwise at the corner point, right sides facing, stitch across diagonally, cut off the excess lace close to the stitching, finish and press open. Then stitch in the insertion: Pin the strip to the right side of the curtain and stitch along the edges. Then cut along the center of the fabric behind the insertion press it back along the seams and stitch again from the right side with small close zigzag stitching. At the corner, cut diagonally into the fabric. Finally, trim off the excess fabric close to the edge of the stitching.

Curtains with printed border

The border is 6 cm ($2\frac{1}{2}''$) wide and is positioned 13 cm ($5''$) away from the inner side edge and the hem. Measure the required length and cut strips from printed cotton fabric with a 1 cm ($\frac{3}{8}''$) seam allowance. Stitch the strips together until the required length is reached, mitering the corner with a diagonal seam. Press under the seam allowance and pin the border to the curtain. Stitch close to the edge. Wide ribbon or braid can be used as an alternative.

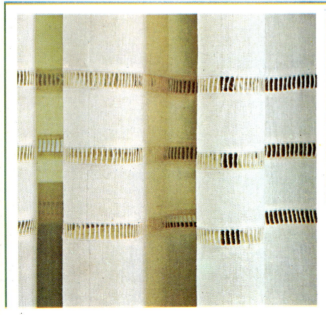

Curtains with narrow braid insertion

This braid insertion is 1.5 cm ($\frac{5}{8}''$) wide. The raw ends are finished before being stitched in. The first row is 10 cm ($4''$) from hem. Cut across curtain at 10.5 cm ($4\frac{1}{4}''$) and insert the braid, stitching it close to the edge. The next band of braid is 5 cm ($2''$) away from the first band. Insert it in the same way. We arranged the bands of narrow braid in groups of three with a 5 cm ($2''$) gap in between each one. The groups themselves are 50 cm ($19\frac{1}{2}''$) apart. The valance has only 2 rows of trimming, the first one 8 cm ($3''$) from the lower edge, the second 5 cm ($2''$) above.

Just checking

Tea towels aren't just for drying dishes. With a little imagination, they can be transformed into curtains, cushions, aprons, a tablecloth, even a tea cozy. So cut off a bit here and add on a bit there for any number of easy-to-make kitchen accessories.

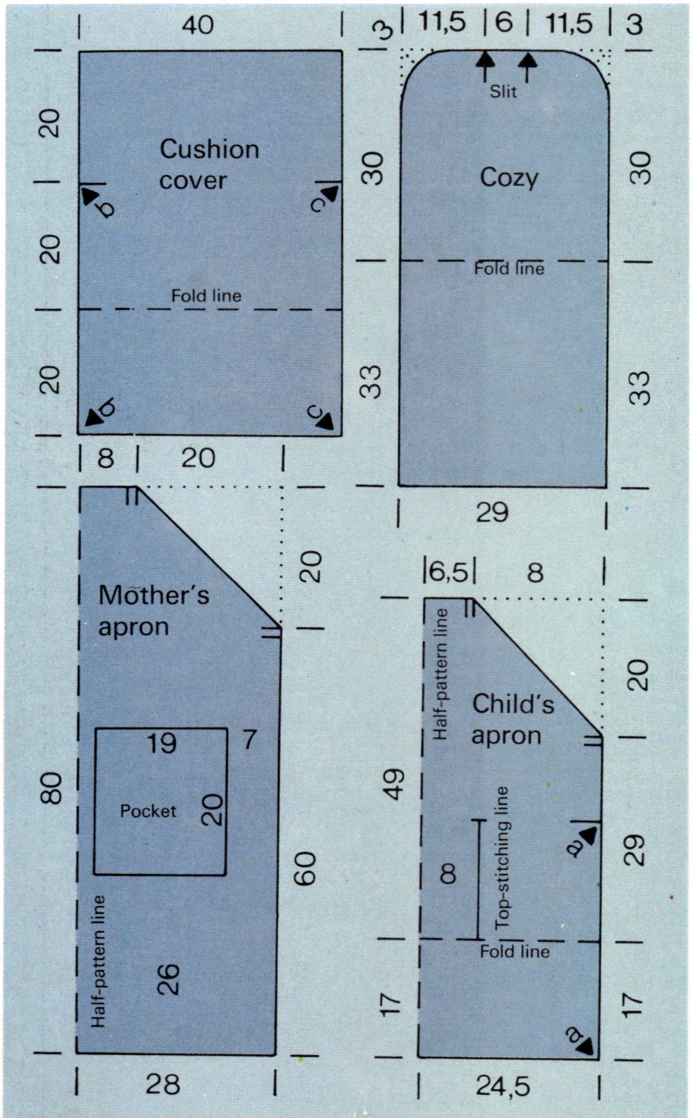

Draw the pattern pieces to the measurements given on the diagram. The numbers are centimeters; inch equivalents are given on the right.

Checked tea towels come in many colors and a variety of sizes. Try to find the most appropriate size for the item you wish to make to avoid unnecessary wastage of fabric. When making articles from several tea towels, make sure that the checks match exactly.

Curtains: Each curtain consists of 2 towels which are sewn together width-wise. To make curtains hang better, remove hem stitching where they are to be joined and trim. Then stitch seam. We stitched tape at upper edge and attached rings to slide along a wooden pole.

Cushion cover: Size of our cushion: 40 cm (15¾") square. Adjust to size of your cushion if necessary or make a cushion. Cut out back 40 cm (15¾") square, plus 1 cm (⅜") seam allowance. Cut front according to the diagram, plus seam allowance all around, leaving one of the towel hems at lower edge (b–c). Place front and back together, right sides facing, and fold the 20 cm (8") front strip onto back, right side to wrong side. Stitch pieces together around other 3 sides. Finish cut edges and turn to right side.

Tablecloth: Adjust the size according to your table. We used 4 cloths measuring 58 cm (23") square. Remove hem stitching on sides to be sewn together to avoid unnecessary bulk here. Stitch 2 cloths each together first, then join center seam.

Napkin: This is 30 cm (12")

square or according to size of cloth. Try to make 2 or 4 napkins from one cloth. Turn edges in twice and stitch.

Cozy: Pattern is given on diagram. Cut it out twice in fabric with 1 cm (⅜") seam allowance all around. If you are using a small cloth, make a seam along fold line. Stitch pieces together along long sides, right sides facing. Finish seams and raw edge at base. Stitch down seam allowance along both sides of slit. Turn cozy. Cut out part above fold line twice in batting or wadding and stitch together, close to edge, around long sides, leaving slit open. Place inside cozy, turn fabric to inside along fold line and draw edges through slit at top.

Aprons: The patterns are given on the diagram. The Child's is to fit a 6-year-old. At the diagonal edge, add 1 cm (⅜") seam allowance, turn back, and finish with seam binding. Position towel hems at top, bottom, and side edges if possible. If not, add seam allowance and finish as for diagonal edges.

Mother's apron: Pocket: Use a remnant from another item, otherwise it can be excluded. For tie bands, cut 4 pieces of tape each 65 cm (25½") long and sew them under at neck and waist corners.

Child's apron: Remove hem stitching at side and lower edges. Refold lower edge hem twice to right side and stitch down. Finish sides. Turn 17 cm (6¾") along fold line to right side for pocket, matching points **a**. Turn seam allowance at sides to wrong side and stitch down. The turned-up section is divided into 3 parts; top-stitch along marked lines. For tie bands, cut 4 pieces of tape 50 cm (19½") long and sew under at neck and sides.

Inch equivalents:

3 cm = 1⅛"	24.5 cm = 9¾"
6 cm = 2⅜"	28 cm = 11"
6.5 cm = 2⅝"	29 cm = 11⅜"
7 cm = 2¾"	30 cm = 11¾"
8 cm = 3⅛"	33 cm = 13"
11.5 cm = 4⅝"	40 cm = 15¾"
17 cm = 6¾"	60 cm = 23⅝"
19 cm = 7½"	80 cm = 31½"
20 cm = 7⅞"	

Pretty and practical
Give your home a face lift

Roller blinds are an attractive alternative to curtains and are often more practical for kitchen and bathroom windows or windows of an awkward shape. The most suitable fabrics are smooth, firm ones such as linen, canvas, and cotton, although finer fabrics can be successful if handled with care. Plastic fabrics are ideal for kitchens and bathrooms as they withstand splashes and can be wiped clean. Loosely-woven or very thick fabrics should be avoided.

Roller blind kits are available complete with a roller, a lath for the lower edge, brackets, and fittings. To calculate the width required, decide first whether it is to hang inside or outside the window recess. If it hangs inside the recess, measure the recess area. If it is to hang outside, add about 15 cm (6″) to the outside measurement of the window frame. The fabric width should be about 2.5 cm (1″) less than the roller, so that it does not catch on the brackets at either side. For the length, add 8–10 cm (3–4″) to allow for the roller and 4–5 cm (1½–2″) for the lath casing. When making up the blind, be sure to fix it to the roller the correct way. Usually the fabric hangs close to the window and behind the roll, but, with special brackets, the position of the spring can be altered to allow the fabric to roll the other way. The 'acorn' or ring by which the blind is pulled down may be attached to the lath or to the casing with a cord or a strip of matching fabric.

Making the blinds

1: Materials Required: Main fabric: Cotton/linen mixture to fit width of window. Insertion: Strips of cotton lace.

Cut out the main fabric to size, allowing 1 cm (⅜″) at each side and at the lower edge, and 8–10 cm (3–4″) at the upper edge. For the lath casing, cut a strip of fabric, 8 cm (3″) wide and long enough to fit the width of the blind plus 2 cm (¾″) seam allowance. Pin the strips of lace insertion at regular intervals to the right side of the fabric and stitch along the outer edges. From the wrong side, cut the fabric behind the lace centrally up its length and press apart. Stitch over the edges from the right side, this time with zigzag stitch, then cut away the fabric close to the stitching on the wrong side.

Finish the raw edges at the top and sides with zigzag stitch. Turn the sides under once and stitch down. On the casing for the lath, press under 1 cm (⅜″) on the short sides. Stitch to the blind, right sides together, with a 1 cm (⅜″) seam allowance. Fold the casing in half, turning under the seam allowance at the back. Stitch down 0.5 cm (¼″) from the seam allowance fold edge.

2: Materials Required: Striped canvas or ticking.

Cut out the fabric as given for the main fabric for Style 1. Then calculate the number of complete scallops required for the width of one window.

Make a template for one scallop and mark the scallops along the edge of the fabric. Add a 0.5 cm ($\frac{1}{4}$") seam allowance at the lower edge. Cut a facing for the scalloped edge, wide enough to form a case for the lath at the upper edge of the scallops. Finish the upper edge, the sides, and the casing with zigzag stitch. Turn under sides and stitch. Stitch the facing to the scalloped edge right sides together and turn to the right side. Join the upper edge of the casing to the blind.

3: Materials Required:
Flower-printed cotton.
Allow an extra 1 cm ($\frac{3}{8}$") at the sides, 4 cm ($1\frac{5}{8}$") for the hem and 8–10 cm (3–4") at the top. Finish the raw edges at sides and top. Turn the sides under and stitch. Make a casing 3 cm ($1\frac{1}{4}$") wide for the lath and attach as for Style 1.

4: Materials Required:
Cotton lace curtain fabric.
Cut out as for main fabric, Style 1, allowing an extra 8–10 cm (3–4") at the top. The fabric illustrated does not fray if the lace motifs remain intact in cutting out. The casing here is made from a row of motifs. Turn under a hem on each side and stitch to the wrong side of the blind, leaving a scalloped edge of motifs at the bottom. With a fraying fabric, a casing made as for Styles 1 or 3 would be more suitable.

5: Materials Required:
Gingham-check fabric.
Follow the instructions for Style 3.

To secure the fabric initially, stick double-sided adhesive tape to the length of the roller. Remove the paper backing and line up the edge of the fabric with the edge of the tape. Press the fabric down firmly.

Secure the fabric to the roller with closely-spaced tacks, making sure that the fabric will roll up and down in the correct direction for the position of the spring.

Insert the lath into the casing at the lower edge of the blind. The lath ensures that the fabric hangs well and gives a rigid support when raising or lowering the blind.

The brackets are fixed to each side of the window frame. The spring tension at the side of the roller may need to be adjusted at first. The roller blind shown here rolls away from the window, but many roll toward the window.

Make bedtime a delight for your small toddler by trimming a pretty print with white cotton lace.

More ideas for the home in easy-care fabrics

One way to sleep pretty...

Duvets or Continental quilts are becoming increasingly popular with young and old alike. Making a bed is so much quicker and easier and suddenly blankets seem very old-fashioned. Here are some ideas for quilt covers and pillows. Note that the open side is closed with ties to make life even simpler.

The open edge is closed with ties. Note that a wide hem hides the bows when they are tied.

Size: <u>Pillowcase:</u> 48 cm x 76 cm (19" x 30"). <u>Child's Quilt Cover:</u> 100 cm x 135 cm (39½" x 53"). <u>Single Bed Quilt Cover:</u> 135 cm x 200 cm (53" x 79").

Tie closing: The ties are arranged in pairs under the hems — three pairs at the end of the child's cover, and six along the side of the single bed cover. For each tie cut a strip 2.5 cm x 20 cm (1" x 8"). Fold in half lengthwise, turn in raw edges, top-stitch. Attach ties when stitching hems.

CHILD'S BED
Materials Required:
Sheeting: 178 cm (70") wide. <u>Pillowcase:</u> 0.6 m (⅝ yd). <u>Cover:</u> 2.2 m (2⅜ yds). <u>Cotton lace:</u> 3 m (3¼ yds).

Pillowcase: Cut two pieces 48 cm x 76 cm (19" x 30") plus 1 cm (⅜") seam allowance on three sides and 5 cm (2") hem on one short side. Stitch lace to one piece 8 cm (3¼") from one long edge. With right sides facing, stitch case on three sides. Turn to right side; hem fourth side.

Cover: The opening is at the foot end of the cover. Cut two pieces, 100 cm x 135 cm (39½" x 53") plus 1 cm (⅜") seam allowance on three sides and 5 cm (2") hem on one short side. Stitch lace to one piece 18 cm (7") from top short end and second row 6 cm (2½") below. With right sides facing, stitch cover on three sides. Turn, and hem fourth side.

GREEN BED
Materials Required:
Sheeting: 178 cm (70") wide. <u>Pillowcase:</u> 0.6 m (⅝ yd). <u>Cover:</u> 3.5 m (3⅞ yds). <u>False turn-back and ruffle:</u> 0.9 m (1 yd) (contrasting color).

Pillowcase: Cut two pieces 48 cm x 76 cm (19" x 30") plus 1 cm (⅜") seam allowance on three sides and 5 cm (2") hem on one short side. With right sides facing, stitch three sides. Turn to right side and hem fourth side.

Cover: Cut one piece 135 cm x 200 cm (53" x 79") plus 1 cm (⅜") seam allowance on three sides and 5 cm (2") hem on one long side. Cut one piece 130 cm x 135 cm (51¼" x 53") plus seam allowance.

For the false turn-back, cut one piece 70 cm x 135 cm (27½" x 53¼") plus 1 cm (⅜") seam allowance on three sides and 5 cm (2") hem on one short side. For the ruffle, cut one strip 178 cm (70") and one 100 cm (40") long, both 6 cm (2½") wide plus 1 cm (⅜") seam allowance on all sides. Join to make one long strip. Finish seam allowances together, then hem one long edge. Gather the other edge to 135 cm (53"). With right sides facing, and the ruffle in between, stitch turn-back to one 135 cm (53") edge of the shorter cover piece. Open out to make one large piece. Right sides facing, stitch pieces together on 3 sides. Turn. Hem opening.

RED BED
Materials Required:
Sheeting: 4.9 m (5⅜ yds), 178 cm (70″) wide.

Pillowcase: Cut two pieces 48 cm x 76 cm (19″ x 30″) plus 1 cm (⅜″) seam allowance on three sides and 5 cm (2″) hem on one short side. For ruffle, cut two strips 178 cm (70″) long, 8 cm (3″) wide, plus 1 cm (⅜″). Join into a circle. Finish seam allowances, then hem one long edge.
Right sides facing, pin ruffle in small pleats around one pillow piece, pinning it to hem line on fourth side. Baste second piece on top, right sides facing, and stitch around three sides through all layers. Turn to right side. Hem fourth side. Stitch ruffle to upper piece.

Cover: Cut two pieces 135 cm x 200 cm (53″ x 79″) plus 1 cm (⅜″) seam allowance on three sides and 5 cm (2″) hem on one long side. With right sides facing, stitch the cover pieces on three sides. Turn to right side and hem fourth side.

YELLOW BED
Materials Required:
Sheeting: 178 cm (70″) wide. Checked fabric: 4.3 m (4¾ yds). Striped fabric: 0.9 m (1 yd).

Pillowcase: Cut two pieces in checked fabric 48 x 76 cm (19″ x 30″) plus 1 cm (⅜″) seam allowance on three sides and 5 cm (2″) hem on one short side. Cut four right-angled triangles of striped fabric with two

sides measuring 30 cm (11¾″) and long side 44 cm (17⅜″), plus 1 cm (⅜″) seam allowances. Stitch triangles to top piece of pillowcase before assembling as for Green Bed.

Cover: From checked fabric, cut one piece 135 cm x 200 cm (53″ x 79″) and one piece 135 cm x 150 cm (53″ x 60″) plus 1 cm (⅜″) seam allowance on three sides and 5 cm (2″) hem on one long side. From striped fabric, cut a piece 50 cm x 135 cm (20″ x 53″) plus 1 cm (⅜″) seam allowance on three sides and 5 cm (2″) hem on one short side. With right sides facing, stitch striped piece to smaller checked piece. Assemble cover as for Green Bed.

BLUE BED
Materials Required:
Sheeting: 4.8 m (5¼ yds), 178 cm (70″) wide. Cotton edging: 4.1 m (4½ yds).

Pillowcase: Cut two pieces 48 cm x 76 cm (19″ x 30″) plus 1 cm (⅜″) seam allowance on three sides and 5 cm (2″) hem on one short side. With right sides facing, pin edging around one pillow piece, matching raw edge to raw edge, mitering corners and pinning to hem line on fourth side. Assemble as for Red Bed.

Cover: Cut two pieces 135 cm x 200 cm (53″ x 79″) plus 1 cm (⅜″) seam allowance on three sides and 5 cm (2″) hem on one long side. Stitch edging 45 cm (17¾″) from top. Assemble as for Red Bed.

A square deal

Make a patchwork quilt with a difference by padding each square separately. It will then be warm as well as decorative. Use checked fabrics as shown here or a selection of floral prints.

Size: The quilt illustrated, inclusive of ruffle, measures 0.90 m (35½") wide and 1.80 m (71") long. You can make it in any size, but bear in mind that the squares lose about 2 cm (¾") in width and length by filling.

Materials Required: Selection of checked cottons for quilt top (you will need 36 squares; see diagram for

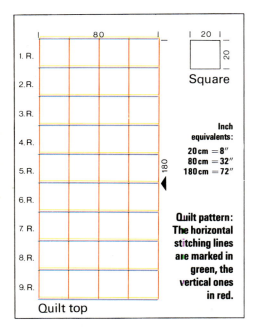

Quilt pattern: The horizontal stitching lines are marked in green, the vertical ones in red.

Inch equivalents:

20 cm = 8"
80 cm = 32"
180 cm = 72"

measurements). Checked cotton: 1.85 m (2 yds), 90 cm (36") wide for underside; 1.60 m (1¾ yds), 90 cm (36") wide for ruffle. Batting or wadding for interlining: 3.30 m (3⅝ yds), 150 cm (58") wide.

Making the quilt

For underside of quilt, cut a piece 80 cm x 180 cm (32" x 72"), plus 1 cm (⅜") seam allowance all around. For the ruffle, cut strips measuring 11 m (12 yds) long in all by 10 cm (4") wide, plus 1 cm (⅜") seam allowance all around.

For quilt top, make a square cardboard template 20 cm x 20 cm (8" x 8"). Cut out 36 squares from checked fabric, adding 1 cm (⅜") seam allowance all around.

Again using the template, cut out 108 squares in interlining without seam allowance. (You will need 3 squares of interlining to fill each square of fabric).

Sort out the fabric squares according to design and color and plan the arrangement. Stitch together 4 squares at a time, and press seam allowances to one side. Stitch the separate strips together. Press the seams as before. Place the top and underside of the quilt together, wrong sides facing. Baste both layers of fabric together on the long sides. First stitch one center horizontal line (see green line marked with arrow on diagram). Then stitch all vertical lines (see red lines on diagram). Fill the center row of 4 squares with the interlining, then close these squares by stitching the quilt together along the next horizontal line (see next green line on diagram). Baste, stitch, and fill the remaining squares in the same way, working from the center to end in one direction, then from the center to the other end.

Stitch the ruffle strips together and join to a circle. Press the seam allowance under twice along one long side and stitch down. Gather the other side to the required length. Stitch the ruffle, right sides facing, to the top and finish the seams together. Fold ruffle down and top-stitch close to edge.

For a comfortable life

RUG

Keeping economy in mind, make the rug with strips of fabric scraps or buy remnants of cheap cotton from department stores. You can vary the size of the rug, but remember that the length will decrease slightly when you work the lines of quilting.

Size: Approximately 120 cm x 235 cm (47¼" x 92½").

Materials Required: Fabric: For top of rug: various cotton fabrics, plain and printed; for rug backing: plain fabric 2.45 m (2¾ yds), 150 cm (60") wide. Strips of fabric for binding the edges: 2 strips 120 cm (47¼") long and 2 strips 245 cm (96½") long, each 8 cm (3") wide. Batting or wadding for interlining: 2.45 m (2¾ yds), 150 cm (60") wide.

Making the rug

Cut out one layer of interlining and one piece of backing fabric to the overall measurements for the rug. Sort out the various fabrics for the top of the rug according to pattern and color. In all, cut out 22 strips, following the measurements on the diagram and adding 1 cm (⅜") seam allowance to the long sides. Stitch these strips together and press seam to one side.

Sandwich the layer of interlining between the top fabric and the backing, wrong sides facing and open-edged. Baste through all layers of fabric around the edge of the rug and along each strip. Stitch through the seamlines of all strips.

Bind the shorter sides of the rug with the relevant strips as follows: With 1 cm (⅜") seam allowance, stitch the strips to the rug, right sides facing, 3 cm (1⅛") from the edge. Fold the binding over to the back, turn in seam allowance; sew down. Work long sides in same way.

CUSHIONS

Cushion 1: Cut out 2 pieces of plain cotton in overall measurements shown in diagram with 1 cm (⅜") seam allowance all around. For filling, cut 5 layers of batting or wadding to same dimensions, but without seam allowance. Baste a layer of filling against wrong side of cushion front. Stitch along vertical stitching lines (see diagram).

Cushion 2: Following measurements on diagram, cut out one piece of plain fabric for cushion back and several strips for cushion front with 1 cm (⅜") seam allowance all around. For filling, cut 5 layers of batting or wadding without seam allowance. Stitch the fabric strips together and press seams to one side. Baste a layer of filling against the wrong side and stitch through the seamlines.

Cushion 3: Following measurements on diagram, cut out 1 piece each of plain and printed cotton with 1 cm (⅜") seam allowance all around. For filling: cut 5 layers of batting or wadding without seam allowance. Baste a layer of filling against cushion front and stitch along horizontal stitching lines.

Cushion 4: For cushion back, cut out one piece of plain cotton in given measurements with 1 cm (⅜") seam allowance all around. For front border, cut 4 strips in plain cotton each 40 cm (15¾") long and 5 cm (2") wide with 1 cm (⅜") seam allowance all around. For center, cut one square in plain cotton and one printed strip according to measurements on diagram, plus 1 cm (⅜") seam allowance. For filling, cut 5 layers of batting or wad-

ding without seam allowance. Miter corners of 4 edge strips. Press under seam allowances of the long sides of printed strip and stitch strip onto center square as shown in diagram. Press under seam allowance of the square and stitch onto the border. Baste a layer of filling to wrong side and stitch through the seamlines.

Cushion 5: Following diagram, cut out 2 pieces of plain cotton with 1 cm (⅜") seam allowance all around and 5 layers of batting or wadding without seam allowance for filling. Baste the top piece of fabric to a layer of filling and stitch the pattern of squares as shown on diagram.

Finishing: Stitch all covers together and turn, leaving opening for filling. Fill and sew up opening by hand.

◄ **Diagram: Cut out the fabric and interlining to the measurements shown. Numbers are centimeters; inch equivalents are given.**

Inch equivalents: 1 cm = ⅜"; 3 cm = 1⅛"; 4 cm = 1⅝"; 4.5 cm = 1⅞"; 5 cm = 2"; 7 cm = 2⅞"; 8 cm = 3⅛"; 8.5 cm = 3⅜"; 9 cm = 3½"; 10 cm = 3⅞"; 11 cm = 4⅜"; 12.5 cm = 5"; 13 cm = 5⅛"; 14 cm = 5½"; 15.5 cm = 6⅛"; 16 cm = 6¼"; 16.5 cm = 6½"; 17 cm = 6⅝"; 18 cm = 7⅛"; 18.5 cm = 7⅜"; 20 cm = 7¾"; 21 cm = 8¼"; 30 cm = 11¾"; 40 cm = 15¾"; 120 cm = 47¼"; 243 cm = 95⅝".

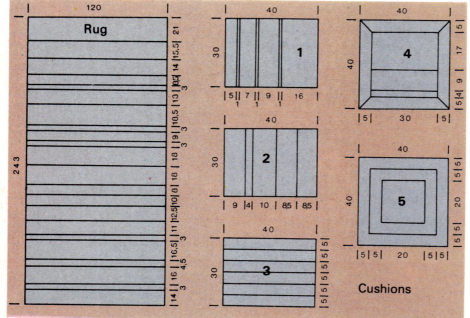

Here's a soft, quilted rug for any room which needs a little color and warmth. It's made of strips of cotton. Any extra fabric can be used for matching cushions.

Another bright idea for your home

Materials Required:
Ribbons. Cushions 40 cm (16″) square. Backing fabrics 44 cm (17½″) square. Cardboard.

Making the cushions
Stitch the ribbons together as directed. Cut out a template and then cut out the ribbons, adding 1 cm (⅜″) seam allowance on all edges. Arrange the pieces as illustrated and stitch.

Cushion 1: Stitch ribbons together to form a piece 30 cm (12″) by 120 cm (48″). Draw and cut a template 20 cm (8″) square. Fold the ribbons in half crosswise. Draw a diagonal line joining two corners of the template and place it along the ribbon stitching. Rotate the template so that the line is at a slight angle to the stitching. Cut through both layers. Cut the other two squares so that they match the first two exactly. Arrange the squares so that the ribbons form a diamond.

Cushions 2 and 3: Stitch the ribbons together to form a piece 160 cm (64″) by 22 cm (8¾″). Cut a template 40 cm (16″) square. Fold it diagonally and diagonally again to form right-angled triangles. Cut 4 triangles.

Cushion 4: Stitch the ribbons and cut the template to the same sizes as for Cushion 1. Draw a diagonal line joining two corners of the template. Place the line on the stitching of the ribbons. Cut four squares.

Cushion 5: When stitching the ribbons together, begin with the longest one diagonally across the center, cutting it to 60 cm (24″) in length. Cut the ribbons on either side progressively shorter to form a 44 cm (17½″) square.

Finishing: Cut a backing piece 44 cm (17½″) square. Place the backing and top together, right sides facing, and stitch around 3 sides. Turn right side out, insert cushion, slip-stitch opening.

Country patchwork

Use up all those scraps of fabric you've been hoarding for so long to make a set of traditional patchwork cushions. They are machine-stitched so that they are made quite quickly. Our cushions are mainly floral, giving them a fresh country charm, but experiment with plain or geometric patterns for different effects. Try to use the same weight and quality of fabric for all the patches.

Sizes: Cushion 1 is a circle 48 cm (19″) in diameter. Cushion 2 is a rectangle 42 x 56 cm (16½″ x 22″). Cushion 3 has a side length of 23 cm (9″). Cushion 4 is 40 cm (15¾″) square.

Materials Required: Scraps of fabric of same weight. Backing fabric to match. Thick polyester batting or wadding.

Making the cushions

The hexagonal patch is shown actual-

Fig. 1

Fig. 2

size in the lower right-hand corner. Make a template from cardboard with a 0.5 cm (¼″) seam allowance. Cut out the patches from the appropriate fabric, using the template as a guide. In Cushions 1 and 2, the hexagons are stitched together in rows; in Cushions 3 and 4, they are stitched together in circles.

In rows: Stitch the hexagons together in straight rows as shown in Fig. 1, pressing each seam to one side as you finish

it. Then fit the rows together zigzag fashion. Stitch each seam up to the corner then, leaving the needle in the fabric, lift the presser foot and place the next 2 sides together for seaming. Repeat at each corner.

In circles: First stitch 2 hexagons together, then add a 3rd with one side against each of the other 2 hexagons as in Fig. 2. Keep the 3rd patch on top while stitching. Stitch up one side to the seam, lift the presser foot leaving the needle in the fabric, and place the next 2 sides together for seaming. Continue adding patches to form a circle.

When the patchwork is big enough, cut out the cushion shape with seam allowance. Make a paper pattern piece if necessary. Stitch the front and backing fabric together, right sides facing, leaving an opening for turning.

To make the cushion pad, cut out 4 layers of batting or wadding: 2 the same size as the cushion cover, 2 slightly smaller. Sandwich the smaller layers between the larger ones and overcast the edges together firmly. Stuff the cushion with this pad and sew up the opening by hand.

The hexagonal template is shown here actual size.

4

How does your garden grow?

Keeping your flowers healthy is no trouble if all your gardening tools are neatly arranged in this practical basket lined with sailcloth.

Our lined basket is very practical for all amateur gardeners and would make a much-appreciated gift for plant-loving friends.

The idea is simple — a strip of sailcloth is cut to fit your basket and separate pockets are stitched to it to hold the various gardening hand tools. The strip is fastened to the edge of the basket with ties.

As baskets come in so many shapes and sizes, the pocket strip must be adapted to fit. On straight-sided baskets, the lining is simply a strip the length of the inner circumference, joined by one seam.

On baskets wider at the top than at the bottom, cut the lining as follows: Measure the inner circumference of the basket twice, once around the upper edge and once around the base. The easiest way to do this is to stick adhesive tape inside and then measure its length. Cut out the sailcloth to fit the larger circumference and the height of the basket plus a 1.5 cm ($\frac{5}{8}$") seam allowance all around. Divide this strip into several equal parts (for our circular basket, it was divided into 6) and stitch darts at these points from bottom to top, distributing the surplus width at the bottom equally among them. The seam counts as one of the darts.

Press the seam and darts open on the wrong side and make a 1.5 cm ($\frac{5}{8}$") hem at top and bottom. At the top edge, catch in the center of the ties which are about 50 cm (19$\frac{1}{2}$") long.

Cut out the pockets to fit your tools (see the small photograph), adding 1.5 cm ($\frac{5}{8}$") all around. Stitch under 1.5 cm ($\frac{5}{8}$") along top and bottom. Turn under the seam allowance at the sides and stitch the pockets to the strip, leaving the top and bottom edges open.

Tie lining to basket.

In striped and checked cotton **Practical kitchen cover-ups**

The classic kitchen apron is back again. Prettier than an overall, but more practical than a frilly cocktail apron, the basic style can be adapted in different ways with trimmings such as braid, rickrack, lace, or bias strips.

The apron on the left is trimmed with scalloped braid, the one on the right with inserts of lace.

FOR ALL APRONS

Cutting out: Enlarge pieces to measurements given on the pattern. Add seam allowances. Skirt: waist 1 cm ($\frac{3}{8}$″), sides and hem 2 cm ($\frac{3}{4}$″). Pocket and bib: 1 cm ($\frac{3}{8}$″) unless otherwise instructed. Waistband: 2 strips 4 cm ($1\frac{1}{2}$″) wide, 150 cm (60″) long with 1 cm ($\frac{3}{8}$″) seam allowance all around. Straps: 2 strips 8 cm (3″) wide, 100 cm ($39\frac{1}{2}$″) long with 1 cm ($\frac{3}{8}$″) seam allowance all around.

Sewing: Unless otherwise instructed, turn under hem twice and stitch. Make pleats at waist and tack. Fold and press shoulder straps lengthwise with seam allowances to inside. Stitch, catching in bib. Press under seam allowances on waistband strips. Stitch together, catching in skirt and bib. Stitch on pockets. Shoulder straps are crossed at back; work buttonholes in waistband and sew buttons to straps.

Style 1

Materials Required: Fabric: 2.50 m ($2\frac{3}{4}$ yds), 90 cm (36″) wide. Cotton braid: 3.10 m ($3\frac{3}{8}$ yds).
For hem band, cut a strip 8 cm (3″) wide with a 1 cm ($\frac{3}{8}$″) seam allowance; turn under the 2 long edges. Stitch braid to both edges. Turn lower seam allowance of skirt to right side. Stitch band over skirt matching the checks carefully.
For bands for pockets and bib: cut 2 strips 4 cm ($1\frac{1}{2}$″) wide, 17 cm ($6\frac{3}{4}$″) long and 1 strip 4 cm ($1\frac{1}{2}$″) wide, 22 cm ($8\frac{5}{8}$″) long plus seam allowances. Attach in same way.

Style 2

Materials Required: Fabric: 2.50 m ($2\frac{3}{4}$ yds), 90 cm (36″) wide. Insertion lace: 2.40 m ($2\frac{5}{8}$ yds).
Insert lace. In skirt: 1st row 8 cm (3″) from edge, 2nd row 6.5 cm ($2\frac{1}{2}$″) away. In bib: 1st row 2 cm ($\frac{3}{4}$″) from upper edge, 2nd row 2 cm ($\frac{3}{4}$″) away. In pockets: 1 row 4 cm ($1\frac{1}{2}$″) from edge.

Style 3

Materials Required: Fabric: 2.50 m ($2\frac{3}{4}$ yds), 90 cm (36″) wide. Cotton lace: 1.20 m ($1\frac{3}{8}$ yds).
Add 2 cm ($\frac{3}{4}$″) to upper edge of bib when cutting out. Turn under twice and stitch. Stitch on lace border 3 cm ($1\frac{1}{4}$″) from upper edge. At hem, stitch on lace 10 cm (4″) from edge.

Style 4

Materials Required: Fabric: 1.90 m ($2\frac{1}{8}$ yds), 140 cm (54″) wide.
Hem band, pockets, and bib are all cut on the bias

In the same basic pattern, this apron in butcher boy stripes is trimmed with wide borders of white cotton lace.

On the blue checked apron, the pockets, bib, and hem are cut on the bias to give an interesting contrast.

4

3

with a 1 cm ($\frac{3}{8}''$) seam allowance. Stitch hem band on as for Style 1 (without the braid). Turn under upper edge of bib and pockets and stitch.

Style 5

Materials Required: Fabric: 2.50 m (2$\frac{3}{4}$ yds) 90 cm (36") wide. Trim: Remnant of white cotton.

Cut out the white bands on bib and pockets according to the diagram. Stitch right side of bands to wrong side of bib and pockets. Clip seam allowance and turn. Press seam allowance toward bands, then top-stitch in place.

Style 6

Materials Required: Fabric: 2.50 m (2$\frac{3}{4}$ yds) 90 cm (36") wide. Rickrack.

Large pockets on an apron are very useful. Here the pockets and bib are trimmed with contrasting fabric.

Pattern for skirts: Numbers are centimeters, inch equivalents are: 68 cm = 26$\frac{3}{4}''$; 7 cm = 2$\frac{3}{4}''$; 8 cm = 3"; 14 cm = 5$\frac{1}{2}''$; 17 cm = 6$\frac{3}{4}''$; 11 cm = 4$\frac{1}{2}''$; 6 cm = 2$\frac{1}{2}''$; 9 cm = 3$\frac{1}{2}''$; 21 cm = 8$\frac{1}{4}''$; 10 cm = 4"; 8.5 cm = 3$\frac{1}{4}''$; 5 cm = 2"; 19 cm = 7$\frac{1}{2}''$; 45 cm = 17$\frac{3}{4}''$. Enlarge pattern pieces. Pocket and bib trims are for Style 5 only.

1.60 m (1$\frac{3}{4}$ yds) each of red, white, and blue.
Add 2 cm ($\frac{3}{4}''$) to the upper edge of bib and pockets when cutting out. Turn under the upper edges twice and stitch. Stitch on the rickrack in parallel rows 2 cm ($\frac{3}{4}''$) apart. At the hem, the 1st row is 8 cm (3") from the edge, on the bib the 1st row is 2 cm ($\frac{3}{4}''$) from the upper edge, and on the pockets 1st row is 1 cm ($\frac{3}{8}''$) from the upper edge.

Gingham checks are always fresh-looking. This apron is trimmed with rows of rickrack braid.

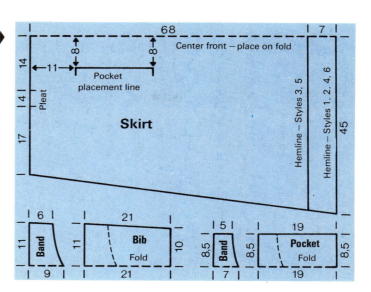

Our pinafore pattern is the simplest imaginable, so it's great fun to sew as you'll finish it in no time. The pinafores also have many other uses, too — as an apron, a house dress, a cool summer dress, or a beach cover-up. If you use a symmetrical check or plain fabric, you can cut out the back and front in one piece. For one-way designs such as the large check illustrated, a shoulder seam is required.

Size: 84 cm–92 cm (33"–36") bust.

Short pinafore
Materials Required:
Cotton: 1.60 m (1¾ yds), 90 cm (36") wide. Iron-on interfacing for shaped neck facing.

Cutting out: Enlarge the pattern pieces to the measurements on the diagram. See cutting layout.
Seam allowances: 4 cm (1½") for hem, 2 cm (¾") at side seams, and 1 cm (⅜") elsewhere.
Cut 2 strips for the casing, each 5 cm (2") wide and 60 cm (23⅝") long. Cut 2 strips for the ties, each 5 cm (2") wide and 95 cm (37⅜") long plus 1 cm (⅜") seam allowance all around. Draw a shaped piece for facing the neck edge by tracing off a strip 3 cm (1¼") wide around the neck as a separate pattern piece. Cut this out in one piece in both fabric and iron-on interfacing, allowing 1 cm (⅜") all around for seam allowance.

Sewing: Finish seam allowances of side seams, armholes, and the casing strips. Iron the interfacing onto the shaped neck facing. Pin, then stitch this around the neck edge, right sides facing. Clip into the corners up to the stitching line and turn the facing to the inside. Baste along the edge and top-stitch close to the edge. Turn

These pinafores in cotton are not only practical, but very pretty too, and simple enough for a beginner to tackle. They are cut wide and straight with high side slits and a tie belt drawn through a casing. So choose a pretty fabric and solve your cover-up problems.

Overall effect

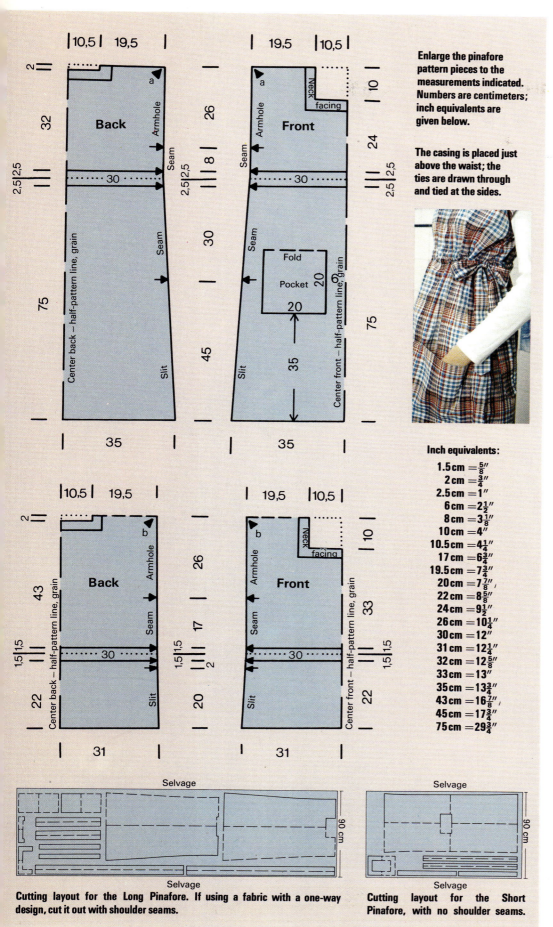

Enlarge the pinafore pattern pieces to the measurements indicated. Numbers are centimeters; inch equivalents are given below.

The casing is placed just above the waist; the ties are drawn through and tied at the sides.

Back — Armhole — Seam — Center back – half-pattern line, grain — Slit

Front — Neck facing — Armhole — Seam — Fold Pocket 20 — Center front – half-pattern line, grain — Slit

Inch equivalents:

1.5 cm	$=\frac{5}{8}''$
2 cm	$=\frac{3}{4}''$
2.5 cm	$=1''$
6 cm	$=2\frac{1}{2}''$
8 cm	$=3\frac{1}{8}''$
10 cm	$=4''$
10.5 cm	$=4\frac{1}{4}''$
17 cm	$=6\frac{3}{4}''$
19.5 cm	$=7\frac{3}{4}''$
20 cm	$=7\frac{7}{8}''$
22 cm	$=8\frac{5}{8}''$
24 cm	$=9\frac{1}{2}''$
26 cm	$=10\frac{1}{4}''$
30 cm	$=12''$
31 cm	$=12\frac{1}{4}''$
32 cm	$=12\frac{5}{8}''$
33 cm	$=13''$
35 cm	$=13\frac{3}{4}''$
43 cm	$=16\frac{7}{8}''$
45 cm	$=17\frac{3}{4}''$
75 cm	$=29\frac{3}{4}''$

Cutting layout for the Long Pinafore. If using a fabric with a one-way design, cut it out with shoulder seams.

Selvage — 90 cm — Selvage

Cutting layout for the Short Pinafore, with no shoulder seams.

Selvage — 90 cm — Selvage

---

under the hem twice and stitch. Join side seams between arrows where marked. Press the seam allowance of the side slits to the inside and stitch down at presser foot width from edge. Stitch down seam allowance of armholes in same way. Press under seam allowance on short ends of casing strips. Stitch these strips to front and back along the marked lines, wrong sides facing, so that the strips end 1 cm ($\frac{3}{8}''$) away from the side seams. Then stitch and turn the ties, top-stitch, and draw through the casing with a safety pin.

Long pinafore
Materials Required:
Cotton: 3.30 m ($3\frac{5}{8}$ yds), 90 cm (36") wide. Iron-on interfacing for the shaped neck facing.

Cutting out: Enlarge the pattern pieces to the measurements on the diagram. See cutting layout.
Seam allowances: 4 cm ($1\frac{5}{8}''$) for hem, 2 cm ($\frac{3}{4}''$) at side seams, and 1 cm ($\frac{3}{8}''$) elsewhere.
For the casing, cut 2 strips each 7 cm ($2\frac{3}{4}''$) wide and 60 cm ($23\frac{5}{8}''$) long. Cut 2 strips for the ties, each 9 cm ($3\frac{1}{2}''$) wide and 150 cm (60") long, plus 1 cm ($\frac{3}{8}''$) seam allowance. Cut 2 more strips each 75 cm (30") long, plus seam allowance. Using the pattern as a guide, draw shaped pieces 3 cm ($1\frac{1}{4}''$) wide for the neck facing, one for the back and one for the front. Cut out with 1 cm ($\frac{3}{8}''$) seam allowance in both fabric and interfacing. Cut out pocket twice with a center fold and 1 cm ($\frac{3}{8}''$) seam allowance.

Sewing: Join shoulder seams, then follow instructions for the Short Pinafore. Stitch and turn the pockets and stitch on where marked before joining side seams. Sew a long and a short strip together for each tie.

Overblouse with kimono sleeves

Easy to sew in stripes

1

These short overblouses with kimono sleeves and a tie belt are ideal to wear with pullovers and T-shirts. They are very simple to make — even for beginners.

Take care with the direction of the stripes when cutting out this overblouse – they are horizontal on the shoulder pieces. There are no fastenings, just side slits and a tie belt.

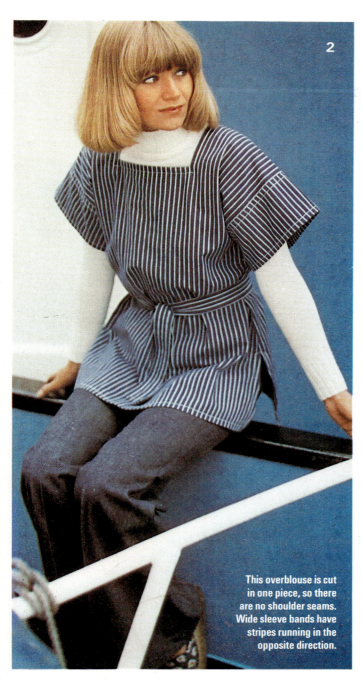

This overblouse is cut in one piece, so there are no shoulder seams. Wide sleeve bands have stripes running in the opposite direction.

The pattern here is cut on the bias to achieve diagonal stripes. It has a center front and back seam and, in contrast to the others, a V-neck.

Size: Small pattern fits 84 cm (33") bust. Large pattern fits 92 cm (36") bust.

STYLE 1
Materials Required:
Striped fabric: 2.40 m (2⅝ yds), 90 cm (36") wide. Thread.

Cutting out: Enlarge the pattern from the graph. Trace the front and back up to the shoulder. Trace the complete shoulder piece. Add seam allowances given below.

Seam allowances: Add 2 cm (¾") for the hem. For side seams, add 2 cm (¾"). Add 1.5 cm (⅝") to all other edges.

Neck facing: The neck edge is faced with shaped pieces of fabric not shown on the graph. To make the pattern pieces, draw a line parallel to neck edge on back and front, about 3 cm (1¼") away. Trace around this line and the neck edge and add seam allowances. Place the pieces on the fabric so that the center front and back lie along the center of a stripe and there is enough room for the belt.

Tie belt: Cut 2 tie belt strips, each measuring 8 cm (3") wide and 90 cm (36") long, plus seam allowance. Cut out.

Sewing: Stitch shoulder piece to front and back. Finish seam allowances together and press toward shoulder. Stitch facing pieces together; pin to neck edge, right sides together. Stitch and turn. Top-stitch around neck edge 1 cm (⅜") from the edge.
Join side seams as far as slits. Finish seam allowances. Turn under hem and raw edges at slit and top-stitch as for neck. Turn under sleeve hem and top-stitch.
To make the tie belt, stitch strips together, right sides facing, turn, and top-stitch.

STYLE 2
Materials Required:
Striped fabric: 3.30 m (3⅝ yds), 90 cm (36") wide. Thread.

Cutting out: Enlarge the pattern from the graph. Trace the pieces. For seam allowances, neck facing, and tie belt, see Style 1.

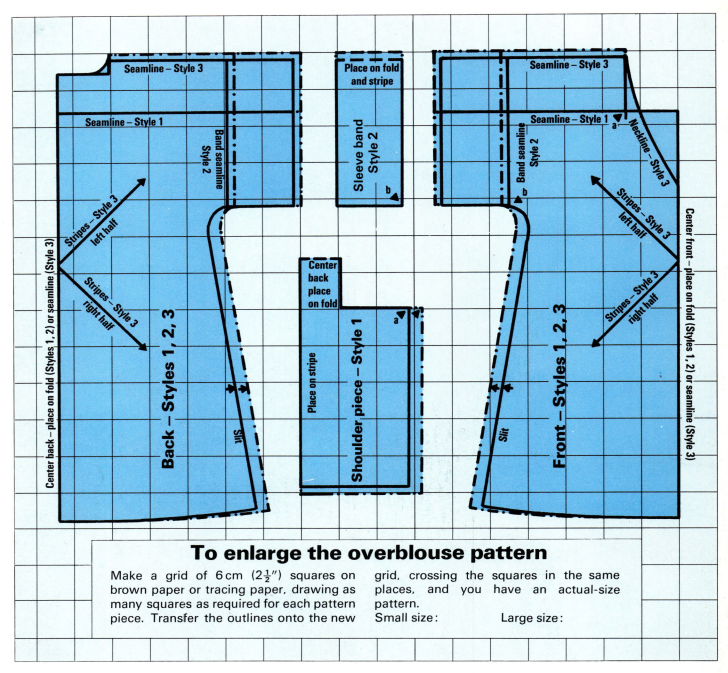

Seamline – Style 3

Seamline – Style 1

Stripes – Style 3 left half

Stripes – Style 3 right half

Center back – place on fold (Styles 1, 2) or seamline (Style 3)

Back – Styles 1, 2, 3

Slit

Band seamline Style 2

Place on fold and stripe

Sleeve band Style 2

b

Center back place on fold

Place on stripe

Shoulder piece – Style 1

a

Seamline – Style 3

Seamline – Style 1

a

Band seamline Style 2

b

Neckline – Style 3

Stripes – Style 3 left half

Stripes – Style 3 right half

Slit

Front – Styles 1, 2, 3

Center front – place on fold (Styles 1, 2) or seamline (Style 3)

To enlarge the overblouse pattern

Make a grid of 6 cm (2½") squares on brown paper or tracing paper, drawing as many squares as required for each pattern piece. Transfer the outlines onto the new grid, crossing the squares in the same places, and you have an actual-size pattern.

Small size: Large size:

Glue or pin the front and back pattern pieces together at shoulder, as front and back are cut in one piece. Place the patterns on the fabric, making sure that center back and front lie along the center of a stripe. Cut out.

Sewing: Stitch facing pieces together. Pin to neck edge, right sides together. Stitch and turn. Top-stitch 1 cm (⅜") from the edge. Stitch sleeve bands to front and back. Finish seam allowances and press toward the band, then top-stitch.

Join side seams as far as slits. Finish the seam allowances.

Turn under hem and raw edges at slit and top-stitch as for neck. Turn under hem at sleeve and top-stitch. To make the tie belt, follow directions for Style 1.

STYLE 3
Materials Required:
Striped fabric: 3.10 m (3⅜ yds), 90 cm (36") wide.
Iron-on interfacing: 0.20 m (¼ yd), 82 cm (32") wide.
Thread.

Cutting out: Enlarge the pattern from the graph. Trace the pieces. For seam allowances, neck facing, and tie belt, see Style 1. Cut out 2 back pieces and 2 front pieces on the bias on the opened-out fabric, so that the stripes run diagonally. Make sure that the stripes will meet and run on at center front and back seams. The direction of the stripes is indicated on the pattern pieces.

Sewing: Reinforce the neck facing with interfacing. Because of the bias cut, stitch seams with zigzag stitch, or stretch the fabric slightly and stitch over tissue paper. Stitch center back and front seams and shoulder seams. Stitch the neck facing pieces together first, then stitch to neck edge, right sides together. Turn and top-stitch 1 cm (⅜") from the edge.

Join side seams as far as slit. Finish seam allowances. Turn under hem and raw edges at slit and top-stitch as for neck. Turn under the hem at the sleeve edges and top-stitch. To make the tie belt, see Style 1.

Cool and casual kimonos

If you are a beginner at sewing, a lightweight kimono is an ideal first project. Start work on it in the morning and you'll be able to wear your finished garment to watch television the very same evening. That's how quick and easy our pattern is. We give one basic shape for adults and one for children, but the shape is wide enough to fit most figures by merely tightening or loosening the belt.

Materials Required:

Woman: Styles with or without shoulder seams: Fabric: 3.80 m (4⅛ yds), 90 cm (36") wide. (Cut from folded fabric.)

Man: Styles with or without shoulder seams: Fabric: 3.50 m (3⅞ yds), 90 cm (36") wide. (Cut from folded fabric.)

Child: Style without shoulder seams: Fabric: 1.50 m (1⅝ yds), 90 cm (36") wide. Style with shoulder seams: Fabric: 1.45 m (1⅝ yds), 90 cm (36") wide. (Cut from single layer of fabric.)

Cutting out: Enlarge the pattern according to the diagram.

The man's kimono is 17 cm (6¾") shorter than the woman's.

Seam allowances: Add 1 cm (⅜") to all edges except front straight edge which has 2 cm (¾") seam allowance. For hem, add 3 cm (1¼") for adults, 5–8 cm (2"–3") for children to allow for growing.

Check the correct length before cutting out. The pattern pieces are straight-sided so they can be placed side by side on the fabric and cut out without wastage.

Front and back can be cut out in one piece without a shoulder seam, but with a seam at center back.

◀ She wears her light-weight kimono floor length. It is so wide and loose-fitting, that it suits all types of figure.

A kimono is ▶ perfect to show off a pretty fabric. Pick a fun print like the ones we have chosen, or splash out with a bold, exotic pattern.

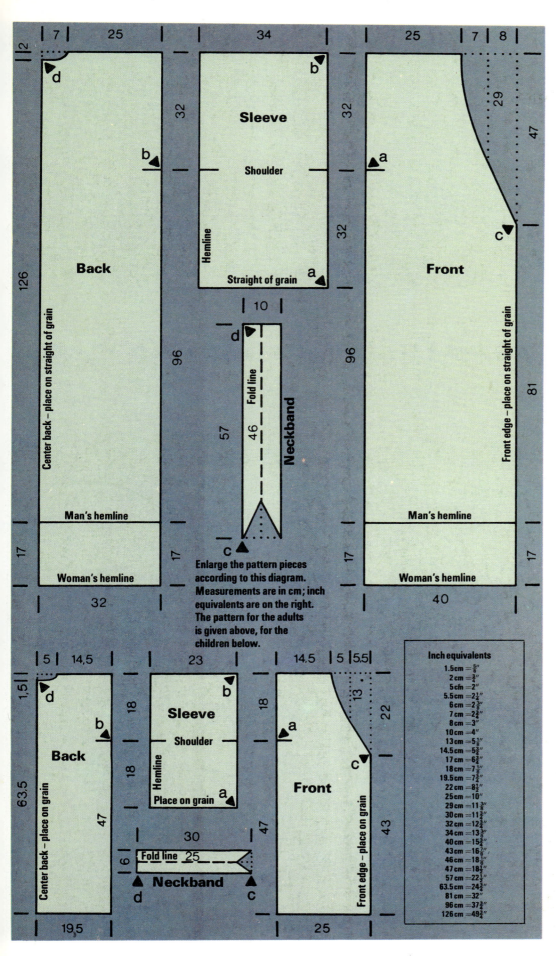

Enlarge the pattern pieces according to this diagram. Measurements are in cm; inch equivalents are on the right. The pattern for the adults is given above, for the children below.

Inch equivalents
1.5 cm = $\frac{5}{8}''$
2 cm = $\frac{3}{4}''$
5 cm = $2''$
5.5 cm = $2\frac{1}{4}''$
6 cm = $2\frac{3}{8}''$
7 cm = $2\frac{3}{4}''$
8 cm = $3''$
10 cm = $4''$
13 cm = $5\frac{1}{8}''$
14.5 cm = $5\frac{3}{4}''$
17 cm = $6\frac{3}{4}''$
18 cm = $7\frac{1}{8}''$
19.5 cm = $7\frac{3}{4}''$
22 cm = $8\frac{1}{2}''$
25 cm = $10''$
29 cm = $11\frac{3}{8}''$
30 cm = $11\frac{3}{4}''$
32 cm = $12\frac{1}{2}''$
34 cm = $13\frac{3}{8}''$
40 cm = $15\frac{3}{4}''$
43 cm = $16\frac{7}{8}''$
46 cm = $18\frac{1}{8}''$
47 cm = $18\frac{1}{2}''$
57 cm = $22\frac{1}{2}''$
63.5 cm = $24\frac{3}{4}''$
81 cm = $32''$
96 cm = $37\frac{3}{4}''$
126 cm = $49\frac{3}{4}''$

However, with a one-way design, a shoulder seam will be required, but no seam at center back.

Cut out the neckband twice on the fold. Tie belt for adults: Cut 2 strips each 130 cm (51") long and 8 cm (3") wide. Tie belt for children: Cut 2 strips 60 cm (23½") long, 6 cm (2¼") wide.

Sewing the kimonos
Join either center back or shoulder seams. Press seams to one side and finish raw edges together. Top-stitch through all thicknesses of fabric the presser foot width away from seamline.

Join side seams by matching point **a** on front to point **b** on back and stitching from hem to this point. Join sleeve seams (narrow sides), press to one side, and finish raw edges together. Turn under sleeve hem 1.5 cm ($\frac{5}{8}$") twice and stitch down. Pin and stitch in sleeve, matching points **a** and **b**. Finish edges together and press toward front or back.

Finish edges of side seams separately and press open. Turn under hem twice and stitch.

Join center back seam of neckband. Stitch together lower diagonal edges, right sides facing, up to seam allowance. Turn and press lengthwise along center.

Stitch 1 long side of neckband around neck opening, right side facing wrong side of kimono. Turn under seam allowance at other edge of neckband, bring it over to right side of kimono, and stitch close to neck edge.

Stitch the 2 parts of tie belt together. Fold belt in half lengthwise, right sides facing, and stitch, leaving an opening for turning. Turn belt to right side and press. Sew opening closed with slip stitches.

Easy-going sewing

Patterns are given in diagram form to fit 88 cm—92 cm (34½"—36") bust, 94 cm—98 cm (37"—38½") hips.
Style 1: White inset stripes are real eye-catchers on the red sweat-shirt.
Style 2: This casual dress with front pocket can be worn with or without long pants.
Style 3: This long version makes a glamorous beach cover-up.

Style 1

Style 3

Style 2

STYLE 1

Materials Required:
Jersey: 1 m ($1\frac{1}{8}$ yds), 159 cm (63″) wide. White jersey: 0.15 m ($\frac{1}{8}$ yd), 159 cm (63″) wide. Remnant of iron-on interfacing.

Cutting out: See cutting layout. Seam allowances: Sleeve hem and hem 3 cm ($1\frac{1}{4}$″), elsewhere 1 cm ($\frac{3}{8}$″).
Shaped neck facing: The neck facing is not included on the diagram. Using yoke piece, draw a facing 3 cm ($1\frac{1}{4}$″) wide to fit neck edge. Cut out with 1 cm ($\frac{3}{8}$″) seam allowance.
Cut out the sleeve bands and bodice bands twice in white with 1 cm ($\frac{3}{8}$″) seam allowance.

Sewing: Use a small, narrow zigzag stitch. First, reinforce the shaped neck facing with iron-on interfacing to prevent the neck edge from stretching. Stitch to neck edge and turn, then top-stitch close to edge. Stitch bodice bands to lower edge of front and back yoke and sleeve bands to sleeves. Press seams open. Stitch sleeves to front and back yoke. Stitch yoke to front and back, matching points **a** then join sides and sleeves in one continuous seam. Finish allowances together. Turn cuff to inside along the foldline, press and sew down. Turn cuff to outside and fasten to sleeve seam with a few stitches. Turn up and sew hem.

STYLE 2

Materials Required:
Jersey: 1.65 m ($1\frac{7}{8}$ yds), 159 cm (63″) wide. Iron-on interfacing: 0.25 cm ($\frac{1}{4}$ yd), 90 cm (36″) wide.

Cutting out: See cutting layout. Seam allowances: Add 3 cm ($1\frac{1}{4}$″) for sleeve hem and hem. At side seams, add 3 cm ($1\frac{1}{4}$″) up to 5 cm (2″) above slit, elsewhere 1 cm ($\frac{3}{8}$″).
Shaped neck facing: See Style 1.

Sewing: Use small, narrow zigzag stitching. First, reinforce the shaped neck facing with iron-on interfacing to prevent the neck edge from stretching. Stitch to neck edge and turn, then top-stitch close to edge. Reinforce one pocket piece with the interfacing. Stitch and turn the pocket and stitch on at top and bottom where marked, 0.5 cm ($\frac{1}{4}$″) from the edge. Stitch through the center twice, 1 cm ($\frac{3}{8}$″) apart. Stitch yoke to front and back skirt, matching points **a**. Press seams toward skirt. Then join sleeves and sides in one continuous seam, leaving the slit open. Finish allowances separately up to about 5 cm (2″) above the slit mark, then together. Press under hem and seam allowances at slit and stitch. Press under hem allowance of sleeve and stitch. Turn back cuff and stitch to sleeve seam.

STYLE 3

Materials Required:
Jersey: 2.05 m ($2\frac{1}{4}$ yds), 159 cm (63″) wide. Remnant of iron-on interfacing.

Cutting out: See cutting layout. Seam allowances: See Style 2. Shaped neck facing: See Style 1.

Sewing: See Style 2, but work the pockets last. Stitch and turn pockets, then stitch on where marked, 0.5 cm ($\frac{1}{4}$″) from edge.

Cutting layouts: From left to right: Style 1, Style 2, Style 3.

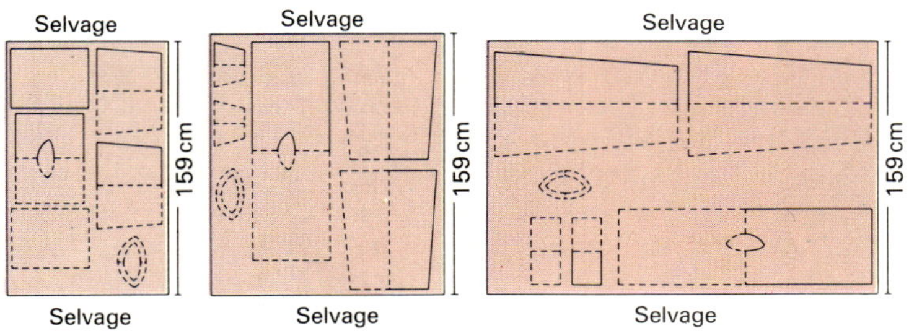

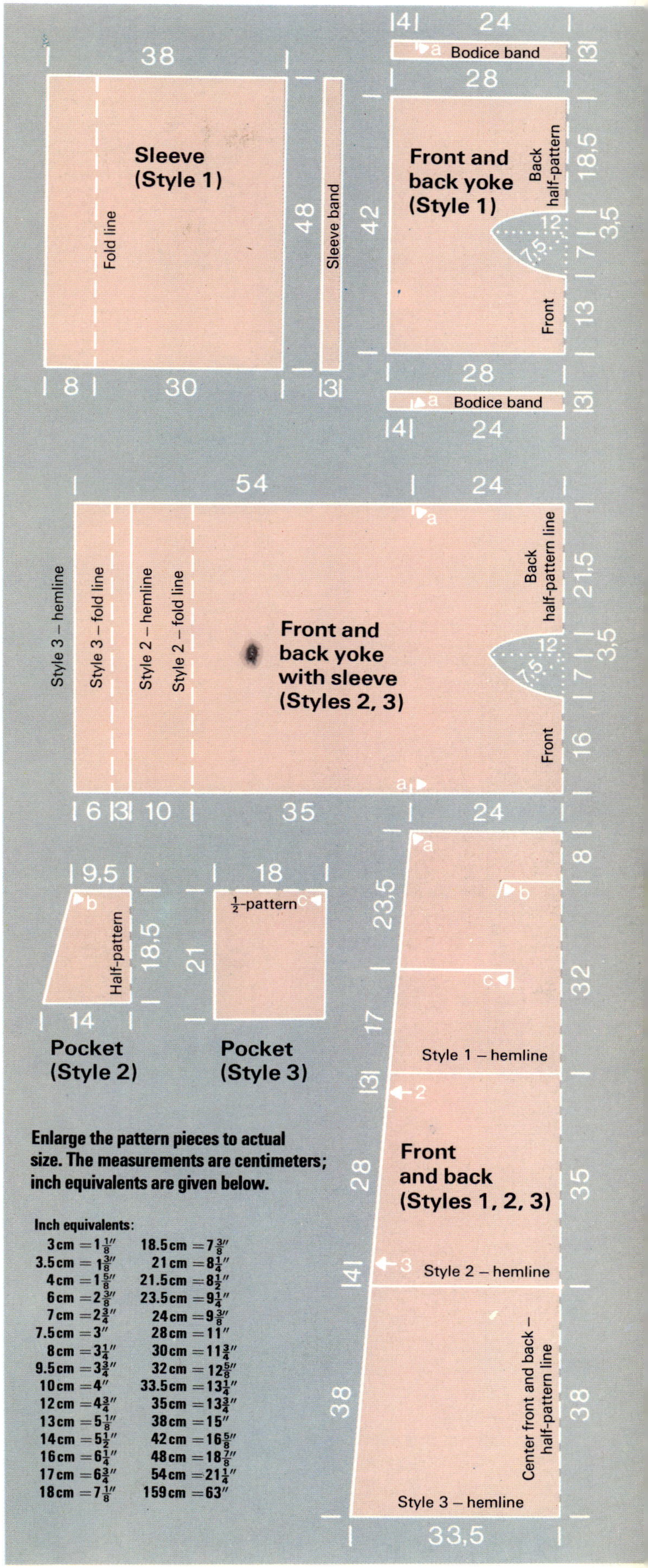

Enlarge the pattern pieces to actual size. The measurements are centimeters; inch equivalents are given below.

Inch equivalents:

3 cm = $1\frac{1}{8}$″	18.5 cm = $7\frac{3}{8}$″
3.5 cm = $1\frac{3}{8}$″	21 cm = $8\frac{1}{4}$″
4 cm = $1\frac{5}{8}$″	21.5 cm = $8\frac{1}{2}$″
6 cm = $2\frac{3}{8}$″	23.5 cm = $9\frac{1}{4}$″
7 cm = $2\frac{3}{4}$″	24 cm = $9\frac{3}{8}$″
7.5 cm = 3″	28 cm = 11″
8 cm = $3\frac{1}{4}$″	30 cm = $11\frac{3}{4}$″
9.5 cm = $3\frac{3}{4}$″	32 cm = $12\frac{5}{8}$″
10 cm = 4″	33.5 cm = $13\frac{1}{4}$″
12 cm = $4\frac{3}{4}$″	35 cm = $13\frac{3}{4}$″
13 cm = $5\frac{1}{8}$″	38 cm = 15″
14 cm = $5\frac{1}{2}$″	42 cm = $16\frac{5}{8}$″
16 cm = $6\frac{1}{4}$″	48 cm = $18\frac{7}{8}$″
17 cm = $6\frac{3}{4}$″	54 cm = $21\frac{1}{4}$″
18 cm = $7\frac{1}{8}$″	159 cm = 63″

Feel free in this flowing caftan. It has a deep front slit and is gathered in by a belt which slots through a casing above the waist. The wide sleeves are cut in one with the main part of the caftan.

This hip-length overblouse is loose and cool for summer. It has short kimono sleeves, side slits, and a bodice which is softly gathered onto a yoke.

Feel free

A soft, flowing caftan and a loose blouse for those long, hot summer days — both are easy and quick to make. They are stunning in glowing prints, preferably those with a border, but if you find it difficult to obtain suitable fabric, you could always improvise with Indian cotton bedspreads, for example, or sew on a separate border.

The caftan is given in sizes B/C, D/E, and F/G, the blouse in size D/E. Enlarge the pattern pieces to the measurements given on the diagram.

CAFTAN

Materials Required:

2 pieces of fabric with border 1.80 m x 1.20 m (71" x 47¼"). Bias binding 0.35 m (⅜ yd), 2 cm (¾") wide.

Cutting out:

Check the length before cutting out, then cut out following the measurements diagram.

Seam allowances: Side seams and hem finish at the borders, so add 1 cm (⅜") here; 1 cm (⅜") at neck; 2 cm (¾") at shoulders.

For the front slit, cut a straight facing strip 8 cm (3") wide and 25 cm (10") long. For the casing strip in front, cut a strip 3.5 cm (1⅜") wide and 22 (25, 28) cm [8½" (10", 11")] long, plus seam allowance. For the tie belt, cut a straight strip or strips to measure 5 cm (2") wide and 118 (128, 138) cm [46½" (50½", 54½")] long, plus seam allowance.

Sewing:

On the front, make 2 slits 2.5 cm (1") long for drawing the tie belt through. Place them just inside the casing strip position and 0.5 cm (¼") down from its top edge as on the diagram. Then turn under allowances of casing strip. Stitch it close to the edges onto right side of front where marked. Join shoulder seams and finish. Pin facing to front over slit, right sides together. Stitch around slit mark and part of neck curve, then cut and turn. Press bias binding slightly into a curve, then stitch to remainder of neck edge and turn. Join side seams, ending at sleeve openings. Press under seam allowance at sleeve edge and hem and stitch down. Stitch front and back together along top-stitching line. Stitch and turn tie belt. Draw it through the casing and the slits from the inside. It is tied at the back.

BLOUSE

Materials Required:

Fabric with border: 1.65 m (1⅞ yd), 115 cm (45") wide.

Cutting out:

Draw pattern pieces, following diagram. See cutting layout. Place pattern pieces widthwise

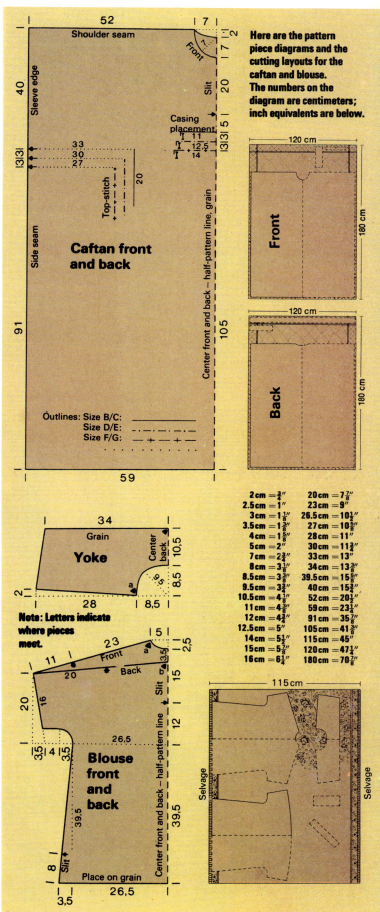

so that the hem of the back and front is on the border.

Seam allowances: Add 2 cm ($\frac{3}{4}$") at sleeve and hem, 2 cm ($\frac{3}{4}$") at side seams tailing off to 0.5 cm ($\frac{1}{4}$") at underarm, and 1 cm ($\frac{3}{8}$") elsewhere.

For the front slit facing, cut a straight strip 8 cm (3") wide and 22 cm ($8\frac{5}{8}$") long. For the mandarin collar, cut a bias strip 5 cm (2") wide and 39 cm ($15\frac{3}{8}$") long, plus seam allowance.

Sewing: Pin the facing over the front slit. Stitch around slit, cut, and turn. Finish all raw edges. Gather the front to 17 cm ($6\frac{3}{4}$") between the ∗ and the neck edge; gather the back to 28 cm (11") between the ∗. Stitch the yoke to

front and back, right sides facing. Turn and top-stitch close to edge. Join the side seams and turn under the seam allowance at the side slit.

Fold the collar in half lengthwise, stitch the short ends and turn. Press the collar into a curved shape as follows: Stretch the raw edge to 41 cm ($16\frac{1}{8}$") and ease the folded edge to 37 cm ($14\frac{5}{8}$").

Stitch one layer of the collar to the wrong side of the neck edge and turn. Turn under the other raw edge and stitch to the right side of the neck edge close to the edge.

Top-stitch all around the slit, and side and top edges of the collar close to the edge. Turn under the sleeve and blouse hem. Stitch.

Sarong style

Size: Small: 84 cm (33″) bust, 90 cm ($35\frac{1}{2}$″) hips. Medium: 92 cm (36″) bust, 98 cm ($38\frac{1}{2}$″) hips.
Materials Required: Printed cotton: 3.00 m (2.75 yds), 115 cm (45″) wide. 2 hooks and eyes.

Cutting out: Enlarge pattern pieces from diagram. Numbers in brackets refer to Medium size.
Top: Cut out on the bias with 1 cm ($\frac{3}{8}$″) seam allowance all around adding the underlap to the left side. For the front tie band, cut a strip 8 cm (3″) wide and 28 cm (11″) long, plus seam allowance.
Skirt: Cut out once on a widthwise fold. Add 2 cm ($\frac{3}{4}$″) for hem, elsewhere 1 cm ($\frac{3}{8}$″).
Sewing: Top: Fold in half lengthwise, right sides facing. Stitch together and turn. Turn in the upper edge 2.5 cm (1″), press, and stitch close to edge. Slant off the ends of the tie band, stitch, and turn. Knot band around the center front of the top to gather it. Finally, sew on 2 hooks at center back and 2 eyes on underlap.
Skirt: Join center front seam and finish edges. Press under seam allowance at upper edge and stitch close to the pressed edge with small zigzag stitching. Trim off the seam allowance close to the stitching. Press under hem and stitch. The front fullness is laid into an inverted box pleat and the corners knotted as shown below.

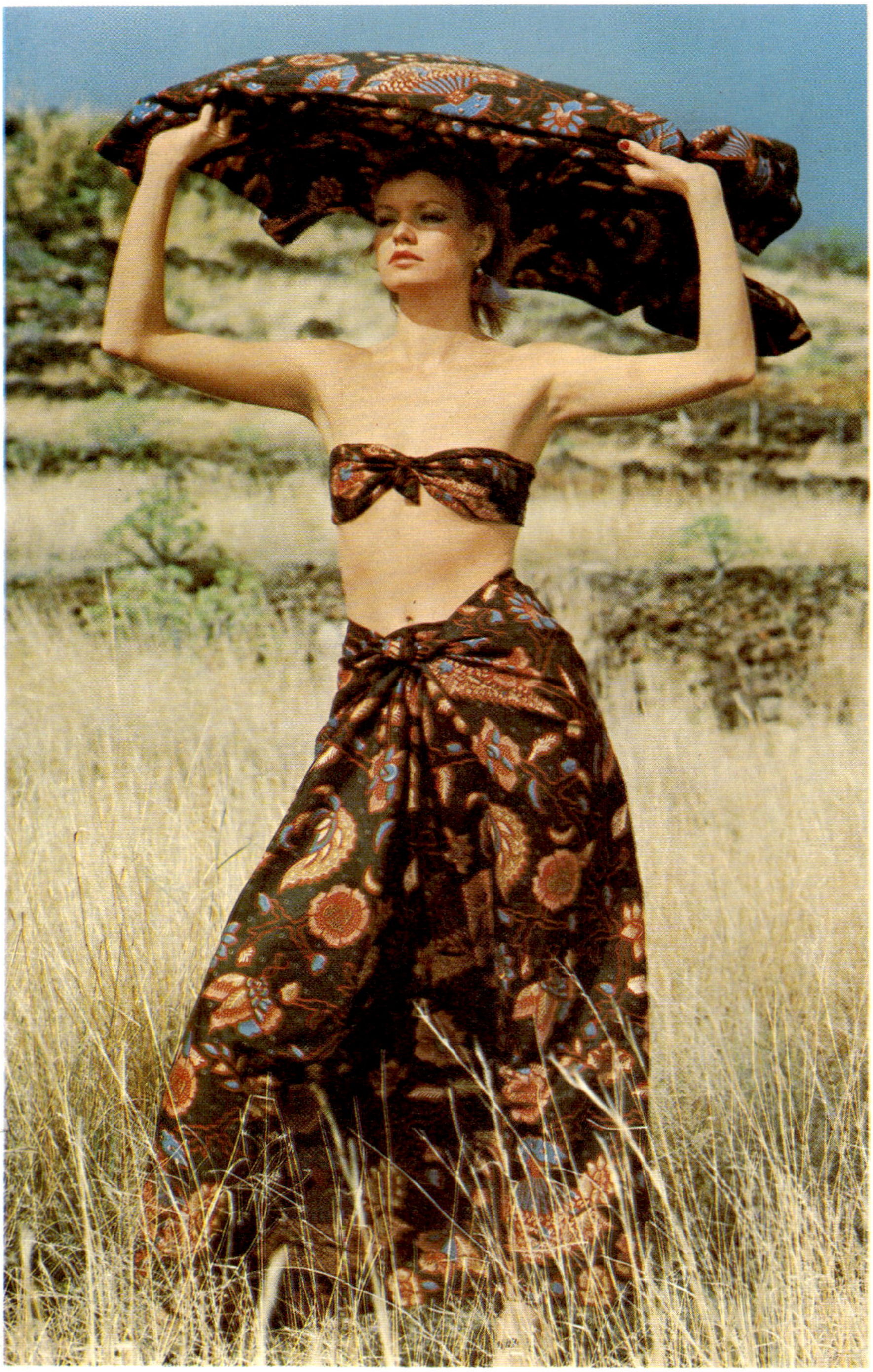

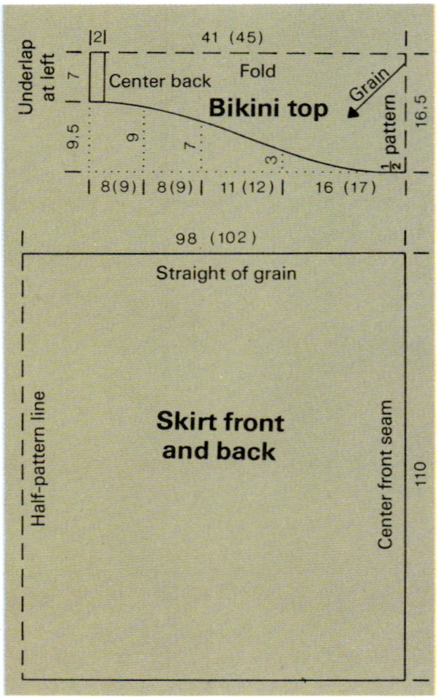

Draw the pattern pieces to the measurements given on the diagram. The numbers are centimeters; inch equivalents are below.

Inch equivalents:

		17 cm = $6\frac{3}{4}$″
2 cm = $\frac{3}{4}$″	9.5 cm = $3\frac{3}{4}$″	41 cm = $16\frac{1}{8}$″
3 cm = $1\frac{1}{8}$″	11 cm = $4\frac{3}{8}$″	45 cm = $17\frac{3}{4}$″
7 cm = $2\frac{3}{4}$″	12 cm = $4\frac{3}{4}$″	98 cm = $38\frac{5}{8}$″
8 cm = $3\frac{1}{8}$″	16 cm = $6\frac{1}{4}$″	102 cm = $40\frac{1}{8}$″
9 cm = $3\frac{1}{2}$″	16.5 cm = $6\frac{1}{2}$″	110 cm = $43\frac{1}{4}$″

Wrap the skirt in front as shown in the diagram and knot the corners.

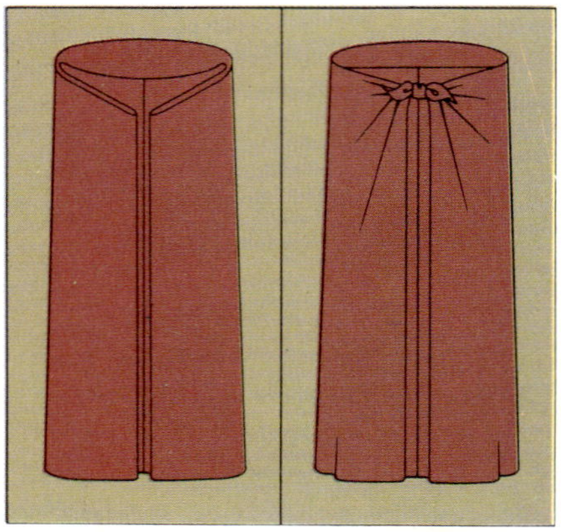

Summer stunners

This stunning beach outfit consists of a bikini and a matching long skirt which can also be worn with other summer tops. The bikini top is knotted at the front and at the neck and then tied at the back. The skirt is fastened at the front with three buttons and the width is gathered in with elastic at the waist to fit comfortably.

Style 1

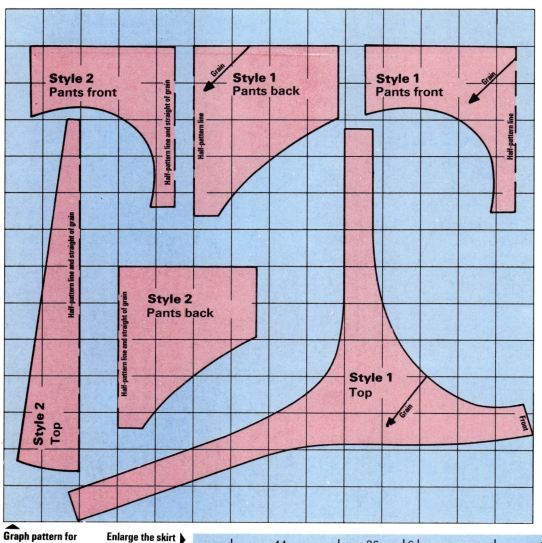

STYLE 1

Size: 92 cm (36″) bust, 98 cm (38½″) hips.

Materials Required: Cotton fabric: 6.70 m (7⅜ yds), 90 cm (36″) wide. Iron-on non-woven interfacing: 0.10 m (⅛ yd), 82 cm (32″) wide. Elastic thread. Narrow elastic: 1.90 m (2⅛ yds). 3 buttons.

Cutting out: Bikini: Cut out all parts on the bias. Top: Cut out 4 times plus 1 cm (⅜″) seam allowance. Pants: Add 2 cm (¾″) at upper edge, 1 cm (⅜″) around legs. Cut a bias strip for each leg 2.5 cm x 60 cm (1″ x 23⅝″).

Skirt: Add 4 cm (1½″) for the hem, 1 cm (⅜″) on other edges. Cut out skirt piece 4 times, the front pieces with cut-in-one facing, back pieces with center seam.

Interfacing: Cut front facing to 2 cm (¾″) below the last buttonhole and 1 cm (⅜″) over the fold line.

Sewing: Top: For each half, stitch 2 parts together, leaving 10 cm (4″) open at the lower edge for turning. Turn and top-stitch close to

Graph pattern for the bikinis: For every square on the graph, draw a square 6 x 6 cm (2⅜″ x 2⅜″) onto paper. Draw the outlines onto the new grid for actual-size pattern pieces.

Enlarge the skirt pattern according to measurements given on the diagram. Draw in the curved hem.

2.5 cm	= 1″
3 cm	= 1¼″
5 cm	= 2″
5.5 cm	= 2¼″
6 cm	= 2½″
9 cm	= 3½″
14 cm	= 5½″
22.5 cm	= 8⅞″
26 cm	= 10¼″
43.5 cm	= 17⅛″
44 cm	= 17⅜″
44.5 cm	= 17⅝″
45 cm	= 17¾″
66 cm	= 26″
67.5 cm	= 26⅝″
94 cm	= 37″
94.5 cm	= 37¼″
108 cm	= 42½″
108.5 cm	= 42¾″

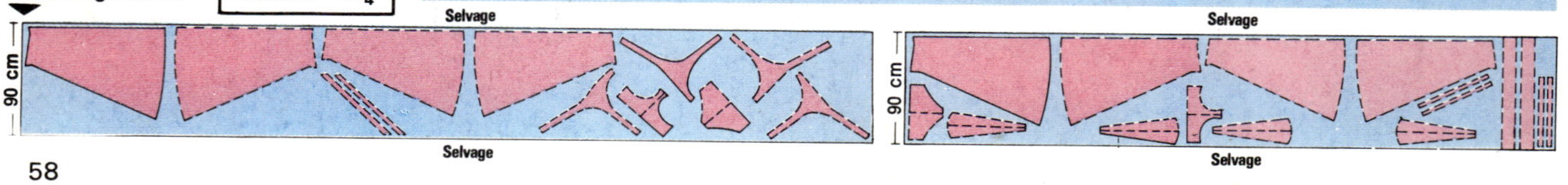

The cutting layout for Style 1 is on the left and for Style 2 on the right. All pieces are cut out of single fabric.

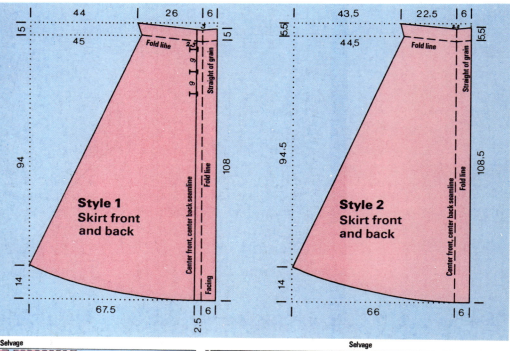

the edge all around. Knot together at the front.

Pants: Join side and crotch seams. Press the bias strips into a slight curve and stitch around the legs, right sides facing. Turn the strip to the inside and stitch, leaving an opening for inserting the elastic. Turn in the seam allowance at upper edge twice and stitch, leaving an opening. Draw elastic through and sew up.

Skirt: Join the side seams; turn the hem under twice and stitch. Press facing to inside along the fold line and sew by hand at hemline. Press under the cut-in-one waistband along the fold line and fasten at the front edge by hand. Top-stitch 0.5 cm ($\frac{1}{4}''$) from front edge. Stitch 5 lines along the waistband, 1 cm ($\frac{3}{8}''$) apart, with elastic thread on the bobbin, stopping 6 cm ($2\frac{3}{8}''$) from the front edge. Draw up the threads and knot together. Make 3 buttonholes and sew on buttons. Sew hanging loops at the sides.

STYLE 2

Size: 88 cm ($34\frac{1}{2}''$) bust, 94 cm (37") hips.

Materials Required: Cotton fabric: 5.20 m ($5\frac{3}{4}$ yds), 90 cm (36") wide. Elastic: 2.5 cm (1") wide, 1.20 m ($1\frac{3}{8}$ yds); 1 cm ($\frac{3}{8}''$) wide, 0.60 cm ($\frac{5}{8}$ yd). Narrow elastic: 1.90 m ($2\frac{1}{8}$ yds).

Cutting out: Top: Cut out 4 times, adding 2 cm ($\frac{3}{4}''$) seam allowance at lower edge, 1 cm ($\frac{3}{8}''$) elsewhere. For casing band, cut 2 straight strips 3 cm ($1\frac{1}{4}''$) wide and 55 cm ($21\frac{5}{8}''$) long plus seam allowances.

Pants: See Style 1.

Skirt: See Style 1.

For waist ties, cut 2 straight strips 10 cm (4") wide and 88 cm ($34\frac{1}{2}''$) long plus seam allowance all around.

Sewing: Top: Right sides facing, stitch 2 pieces together, leaving the lower edge open. Turn. Finish the bottom edges together and

turn under. Stitch $1\frac{1}{2}$ cm ($\frac{5}{8}''$) from the folded edge to form the casing. Stitch the 2 strips for the casing band into 1 long strip, fold lengthways, stitch together, and turn. Insert the 1 cm ($\frac{3}{8}''$) elastic through the casing band. Draw the band through the casing in the top; join into a circle.

Pants: See Style 1.

Skirt: Join side seams. Turn the hem under twice and stitch. Press the facing to the inside along the fold line and sew by hand at the hemline. Top-stitch the fronts close to edge of facing. Press under the cut-in-one waistband along the fold line, turn in the seam allowance, and stitch to make a casing 5.5 cm ($2\frac{1}{4}''$) wide. Cut the wide elastic into 2 strips 60 cm ($23\frac{5}{8}''$) long. Then stitch them together, long edge to long edge, with zigzag stitching. Fold the waist ties lengthwise, right sides facing, and stitch. Turn and stitch the open ends to the ends of elastic. Draw band through casing. Sew loops at sides.

Style 2

On this style, the bikini top is made up of two pieces with a narrow tie band threaded through a casing. The skirt is tied with a bow at the front and left open below this.

The lightweight pants are cut straight and wide. They have a casing at the waist with a tie belt drawn through.

Sizes: Bust 84 cm–88 cm (33″–34½″), hips 90 cm–94 cm (35½″–37″).

Materials Required:
Cotton: Bikini top: 0.55 m (⅝ yd), 90 cm (36″) wide. Skirt: 3.40 m (3¾ yds), 90 cm (36″) wide. Pants: 2.45 m (2¾ yds), 90 cm (36″) wide. Pants and skirt: Elastic: 0.55 m (⅝ yd), 2.5 cm (1″) wide.

Seam allowances: Add 1 cm (⅜″); 4 cm (1½″) to hems.

Cutting out

Bikini top: Cut out 4 times on the bias plus 1 cm (⅜″) seam allowance. For the tie band, cut 2 straight strips 3 cm (1¼″) wide, 88 cm (34½″) long plus seam allowances. For bow, cut a strip 3 cm (1¼″) wide and 30 cm (11¾″) long plus seam allowances.

Skirt: Cut out the skirt panel 4 times, adding seam allowances. For the waist-band, cut a straight strip 6 cm (2½″) wide and 110 cm (43¼″) long plus seam allowances. For the tie belt, cut 2 straight strips 8 cm (3″) wide and 80 cm (31½″) long plus seam allowances.

Pants: Cut the leg section out twice, adding seam allowances. For tie belt, cut 2 straight strips 8 cm (3″) wide and 55 cm (21½″) long plus seam allowances.

Sewing

Bikini top: Join each pair of cup sections at center front, right sides facing. Then stitch the joined pairs together, leaving the sides open for turning. Turn, top-stitch close to the edge and finish the raw edges together. Turn the side edges under along the fold line and stitch to form a 2 cm (¾″) wide casing. Join the 2 strips for the tie

That tropical feeling

with a sun outfit of pants, a skirt, and a bikini top.

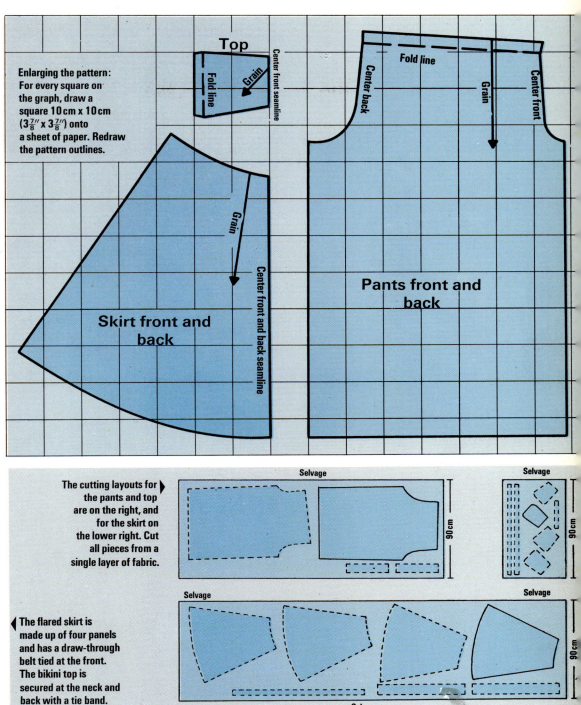

Enlarging the pattern: For every square on the graph, draw a square 10 cm x 10 cm ($3\frac{7}{8}$" x $3\frac{7}{8}$") onto a sheet of paper. Redraw the pattern outlines.

Top
Fold line
Grain
Center front seamline

Fold line
Center back
Grain
Center front

Skirt front and back
Grain
Center front and back seamline

Pants front and back

The cutting layouts for the pants and top are on the right, and for the skirt on the lower right. Cut all pieces from a single layer of fabric.

The flared skirt is made up of four panels and has a draw-through belt tied at the front. The bikini top is secured at the neck and back with a tie band.

Selvage
90 cm
Selvage
90 cm

Selvage
90 cm
Selvage
90 cm

band to one long strip. Fold in half lengthwise, right sides facing, stitch, and turn. Draw the strip through each casing, leaving loop at neck; tie at back.
Stitch and turn the strip for the bow; top-stitch close to the edge. Knot this band over the center front seam.
<u>Skirt:</u> Join center front, center back, and side seams. Turn under the hem twice and stitch. Join the

waistband into a circle and press lengthwise along the center. On top layer of band make 2 buttonholes 2.8 cm ($1\frac{1}{8}$") long, positioning them 2.5 cm (1") either side of the center front. Stitch the waistband to the skirt through both thicknesses, right sides facing, catching in loops for hanging. Finish all seam layers together.
Stitch each tie belt piece,

leaving one short end of each open for turning. Stitch the tie ends to each end of the elastic with zigzag stitching. Draw through the waistband.
<u>Pants:</u> Join the inside leg and crotch seams. Turn the hem under twice and stitch. Turn under the waist along the fold line and press. Make 2 buttonholes, just below fold on right side, 2.8 cm ($1\frac{1}{8}$") long and

positioned 2.5 cm (1") either side of the center front. Now stitch along the waist to form a casing 3 cm ($1\frac{1}{4}$") wide for the tie belt. Stitch each tie belt piece together, leaving a short end open in each for turning. Turn and top-stitch 0.5 cm ($\frac{1}{4}$") from the edge. Stitch the tie ends to each end of the elastic with zigzag stitching. Draw the band through the casing.

Go backless for a super tan

This little top made up in a pretty printed cotton is meant for those really hot summer days. Worn with jeans or cotton skirts, it suits those without too much bust.

This summer top guarantees that you stay cool and expose a maximum of back to the sun. You can make it with or without the decorative frill. The straps tie at the back of the neck, and thin bands at the sides cross at the back and tie at the front.

Size: This teenage top is for girls with a bust measurement of approximately 80 cm ($31\frac{1}{2}$").

Materials Required:
Fabric: 1.2 m ($1\frac{3}{8}$ yds), 90 cm (36") wide. Thread.

Cutting out

Cut out the front twice. For straps, cut two strips measuring 65 cm ($25\frac{5}{8}$") long and for waist bands two strips measuring 1.1 m ($1\frac{1}{4}$ yds) long. Cut all strips 4 cm ($1\frac{1}{2}$") wide plus seam allowances. For frills, cut bias strips measuring 8 cm (3") wide and stitch together for a finished length of 2.5 m ($2\frac{3}{4}$ yds) plus seam allowances.

Sewing the top

The top is double but the two parts are stitched separately and then joined together. Stitch darts. Fold the straps and bands in half lengthwise, right sides together, and stitch one short side and the long side. Turn with the aid of a pencil. For the frills, having stitched the bias strips together for the correct length, fold them in half lengthwise, right sides facing. Turn under the seam allowances on the narrow ends and sew closed by hand. Gather strip along open long side to measure 1 m ($1\frac{1}{8}$ yd) in length and then baste to top and sides of one of the fronts, right sides facing and the fold of the frill towards the garment. Baste the straps and bands in place also. Pin the second front in place, right sides facing, and stitch all around leaving a small opening for turning. Turn to right side, close opening by hand, and top-stitch all around to finish.

---

1 square = 3 cm ($1\frac{1}{4}$")

Strap stitching line

Center front – place on fold on straight of grain

Band stitching line

Front

Enlarging the pattern

Draw a grid of 3 cm ($1\frac{1}{4}$") squares onto brown paper or tracing paper. Then transfer the lines of the pattern from the graph above onto the grid, mark in all instructions, and cut out a full-sized pattern.

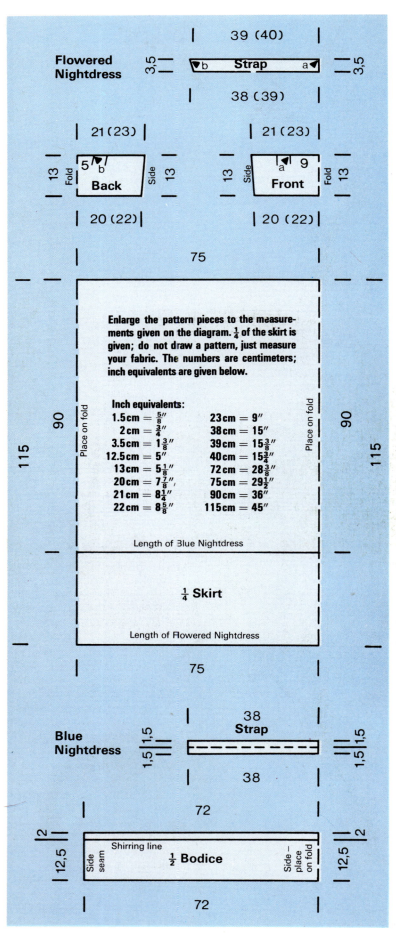

Flowered Nightdress

3,5 — Strap — 3,5
▼b Strap a▼
39 (40)
38 (39)

21 (23)   21 (23)

13 | Fold | 5▼b Back | Side | 13   13 | Side | a▼ Front 9 | Fold | 13

20 (22)   20 (22)

75

115 | 90 | Place on fold ... Place on fold | 90 | 115

Enlarge the pattern pieces to the measurements given on the diagram. $\frac{1}{4}$ of the skirt is given; do not draw a pattern, just measure your fabric. The numbers are centimeters; inch equivalents are given below.

Inch equivalents:

1.5 cm	= $\frac{5}{8}$″	23 cm	= 9″
2 cm	= $\frac{3}{4}$″	38 cm	= 15″
3.5 cm	= $1\frac{3}{8}$″	39 cm	= $15\frac{3}{8}$″
12.5 cm	= 5″	40 cm	= $15\frac{3}{4}$″
13 cm	= $5\frac{1}{8}$″	72 cm	= $28\frac{3}{4}$″
20 cm	= $7\frac{7}{8}$″	75 cm	= $29\frac{1}{2}$″
21 cm	= $8\frac{1}{4}$″	90 cm	= 36″
22 cm	= $8\frac{5}{8}$″	115 cm	= 45″

Length of Blue Nightdress

$\frac{1}{4}$ Skirt

Length of Flowered Nightdress

75

Blue Nightdress

1,5 | 1,5   1,5 | 1,5
Strap
38
38

72

2 — 2
12,5 | Side seam | Shirring line $\frac{1}{2}$ Bodice | Side — place on fold | 12,5

72

Here the border has been shirred for the bodice to complement the border at the hem.

For bed and breakfast

These cool, summery nightdresses are made from border-printed fabrics, incorporating the print into the design. However, they would look equally charming in plain fabric. The blue one has a bodice gathered with shirring elastic and no fastenings. The straps are narrow, the length just below the knee. The flowered nightdress on the right is ankle length. Its straps are made from the edge of the border-print and the neck edge is bound with the same fabric. The skirt is gathered onto the bodice which repeats the design of the hem.

Determine the length of the bodice by the width of your border. To avoid having to cut into the design or add to it, you might have to make the bodice longer or shorter than the ones shown here. The skirt is made from the full width of the fabric with the border along one selvage, forming the hem. The flowered nightdress uses 115 cm (45″) fabric and the blue nightdress 90 cm (36″) fabric.

Size: The bodice of the flowered nightdress is given for an 84 cm (33″) and a 92 cm (36″) bust. The shirred bodice will fit 84 cm–92 cm (33″–36″) busts.

Blue nightdress

Materials Required: Fabric: 4.55 m (5 yds), 90 cm (36″) wide. Sewing thread. Elastic thread.

Cutting out: Skirt: Length = width of fabric (allowing 1 cm ($\frac{3}{8}$″) seam allowance top and bottom). Width = 3 m ($3\frac{1}{4}$ yds). Bodice: See diagram, adjusting depth to suit your fabric. Cut out on the fold with 3 cm ($1\frac{1}{4}$″) seam allowance at neck edge and 1 cm ($\frac{3}{8}$″) at side seam and bottom. Cut straps according to the diagram, checking the length first. Cut out twice on the fold with 1 cm ($\frac{3}{8}$″) seam allowance all around.

Sewing: Join skirt seam and finish allowances. Turn under selvage at hem 1 cm ($\frac{3}{8}$″) and stitch. Finish raw edges of bodice. Turn under the seam allowance at top of bodice and baste. Stitch the first line of shirring 2 cm ($\frac{3}{4}$″) from the top edge, with sewing thread as the top thread and elastic thread on the bobbin. Then stitch a further 7 lines, each about 1.5 cm ($\frac{5}{8}$″) apart. The bodice has a finished width of 30 cm ($11\frac{3}{4}$″). Join the bodice side seam.
Gather skirt to original width of bodice. Stretch

bodice out, pin to skirt, right sides facing, and stitch together with elastic thread. For straps, press under the seam allowances and press in half lengthwise, then stitch along them twice. Stitch straps to bodice at upper shirring line, 8 cm ($3\frac{1}{4}$″) from the center on each side.

Flowered nightdress

Materials Required: Fabric: 4.75 m ($5\frac{1}{4}$ yds), 115 cm (45″) wide. Zipper: 24 cm (10″) long.

Cutting out: Skirt: Length = width of fabric (including 1 cm ($\frac{3}{8}$″) seam allowance at top and bottom). Width = 3 m ($3\frac{1}{4}$ yds). Bodice: See diagram, adjusting depth to suit your fabric.

Cut out front and back on the fold with 2 cm ($\frac{3}{4}$″) seam allowance at side seams, 1 cm ($\frac{3}{8}$″) at waist and none at bodice top. To bind the top edge, cut a strip 2.5 cm (1″) wide and 86 (94) cm [34″ (37″)] long. Cut out straps according to the diagram, checking length first. Cut 4 with 0.5 cm ($\frac{1}{4}$″) seam allowance all around. They are slanted at the back so that they will not slide off the shoulder — the longer side points toward center back.

Sewing: Stitch skirt side seam, leaving an 11 cm ($4\frac{3}{8}$″) slit open at the top. Finish allowances. Turn under the selvage 1 cm ($\frac{3}{8}$″) at the hem and stitch. Gather skirt to width of

bodice, leaving about 2 cm ($\frac{3}{4}$″) straight at zipper. Join right-hand side seam of bodice and finish. Bind neck edge with the strip as follows: turn in the ends, then stitch on the strip, right sides facing, so that the seam allowance of the bodice is 0.75 cm ($\frac{5}{16}$″) and the allowance of the strip is 0.5 cm ($\frac{3}{16}$″). Turn strip to the inside, turn in 0.5 cm ($\frac{3}{16}$″), baste, and stitch down from the right side (or sew by hand along the seamline). For the straps, stitch, turn, and topstitch. Finish the ends and stitch under along the seamline of the binding. Now stitch the bodice to the skirt, right sides facing. Insert the zipper at the side.

This nightdress has a straight bodice which is fastened at the side with a zipper.

Expecting the best

BOTH STYLES

Size: The dress and smock are given in diagram form for an 88 cm (34½″) bust. Enlarge to actual size on tissue paper. To make a pattern for a 92 cm (36″) or 96 cm (37½″) bust, leave the pleated or shirred panel as it is and widen the side parts from 14.5 cm (5¾″) as shown to 15.5 cm (6⅛″) or 16.5 cm (6½″).

DRESS

Materials Required: Cotton fabric: 2.60 m (2⅞ yds), 90 cm (36″) wide. Zipper: 16 cm (6″) long. 4 buttons. Bias binding: 3.25 m (3⅝ yds), 2 cm (¾″) wide. Sewing thread.

Cutting out: See cutting layout. Cut front and back from the same pattern piece with 2 cm (¾″) seam allowance at sides, 4 cm (1½″) at hem, and none at neck edge. Cut out shoulder straps twice with 1 cm (⅜″) seam allowance at slanted back ends and none elsewhere. Round off front ends slightly. Cut out pocket twice without seam allowance.

Sewing: Stitch pleats by placing X onto O and top-stitch close to edge. Join side seams (to arrow only at left) and finish edges. Bind neck edge with bias binding. Insert zipper at left-hand side. Bind straps with bias binding and work buttonholes in rounded ends. Finish back end of straps and stitch on from right side along binding

Selvage

Fold

Selvage

Fold

45 cm

45 cm

Cutting layout for smock (left) and dress (below). Cut in double fabric.

On the smock, the fullness is created by the panels of shirring on front and back. The straps are also gathered up with elastic thread. Pockets are set into the side seams. ▶

◀ The fullness of the dress is held in at the bodice by top-stitched pleats at front and back. All edges are bound with bias binding.

Here you can see the back view of the dress. The shoulder straps are crossed at the back and buttoned in front. ▼

seam. Sew buttons onto front. Turn hem allowance under twice and stitch. Bind pockets and stitch on where marked, stitching along binding seam.

SMOCK

Materials Required: Cotton fabric: 1.90 m (2⅛ yds), 90 cm (36") wide. Sewing thread. Elastic thread.

Cutting out: See cutting layout. Cut out front and back from the same pattern piece with 2 cm (¾") seam allowance at side and neck edge and 4 cm (1½") at hem. Cut out the strap twice and the set-in pocket 4 times with 1 cm (⅜") seam allowance all around.

Sewing: Finish neck edge and press seam allowance to wrong side. Within the area marked, work lines of shirring, parallel to the neck edge and 1 cm (⅜") apart. Use elastic thread in the bobbin and sewing thread on top. Catch in the neck edge

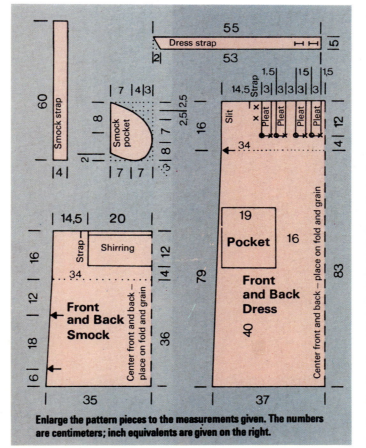

Enlarge the pattern pieces to the measurements given. The numbers are centimeters; inch equivalents are given on the right.

seam allowance with the top line of stitching.
Finish edges of straps and press seam allowance to inside. Stitch close to edges and twice along the center with elastic thread in bobbin. Finish the straight edge of the pocket pieces and stitch to front and back pieces where indicated, right sides facing. Press toward side seam. Finish side seam allowances and join seams above and below pocket opening. Join pocket pieces, right sides facing. Turn up hem allowance twice and stitch.
Stitch straps on at top edge where marked.

Inch equivalents:

1.5 cm = ⅝"	8 cm = 3⅛"
2 cm = ¾"	9 cm = 3½"
2.5 cm = 1"	9.5 cm = 3¾"
3 cm = 1⅛"	10 cm = 3⅞"
3.5 cm = 1⅜"	10.5 cm = 4⅛"
4 cm = 1⅝"	17 cm = 6¾"
4.5 cm = 1¾"	17.5 cm = 7"
5 cm = 2"	18 cm = 7⅛"
5.5 cm = 2¼"	22 cm = 8⅝"
6 cm = 2⅜"	38 cm = 15"
7.5 cm = 3"	90 cm = 36"

Russian accent

Cut a dash in this prettily-trimmed smock dress. The width is held in at waist and wrists by the braid belt and cuffs. Choose a floral braid to tone with the fabric.

Size: 92 cm (36″) bust, 98 cm (38½″) hips and 100 cm (39½″) bust, 106 cm (42″) hips. Enlarge the pattern pieces to actual size on tissue paper.

Materials Required:
Both: Poplin: 3.65 cm (4 yds), 90 cm (36″) wide. Iron-on interfacing for the stand-up collar. 1 toggle and round elastic for the toggle fastening. 2 large press studs or snaps. Smaller size: Floral braid: 1.70 m (1⅞ yds), 6 cm (2½″) wide. Cotton braid binding: 1.90 m (2⅛ yds), 1 cm (⅜″) wide. Larger size: Floral braid: 1.80 m (2 yds), 6 cm (2½″) wide. Cotton braid binding: 2 m (2¼ yds), 1 cm (⅜″).

Cutting out: See cutting layout. Cut out front and back with 1 cm (⅜″) seam allowance at shoulder and sleeve seam, 2 cm (¾″) at side seam and hem. Cut out sleeve with 1 cm (⅜″) allowance all around. Cut out stand-up collar 4 times in fabric and twice in interfacing with 1 cm (⅜″) seam allowance at neck seam and none elsewhere. Iron the interfacing onto 2 collar pieces. Cut out pocket lining 4 times with 1 cm (⅜″) allowance all around. For sleeve slits, cut 2 bias strips 2 cm (¾″) wide and 14 cm (5½″) long. Cut out shoulder yokes and cuffs from braid, and the belt according to your waist measurement.

Sewing: Finish the following cut edges: the side and yoke edges of front and back, the armhole and cuff edges, and the straight edges of the pocket linings. With right sides facing, stitch the straight edges of the pocket linings to front and back where marked. Press pocket linings toward seam allowance. Join side seams, leaving slits and pockets open. Join pocket linings and finish seams together. Press hem allowance under twice and stitch. Press seam allowance of side slits to inside and stitch. Gather fronts along yoke seamline to 8 cm (3⅛″) for smaller size and 9 cm (3½″) for larger size. Stitch the braid yoke, close to edge, onto front and back, wrong side to right side. For the slit on the front, draw a line 1 cm (⅜″) away from the center on each side. Cut along the center and clip diagonally into the corners of marked lines.

Join center back seam of stand-up collars. Pin one collar, without interfacing, to neck edge, right sides facing. Pin the other one to inside neck edge, right side to wrong side, and stitch collars and neck edge together in one seam. Press upward and baste outer edges together.

Bind collar and slit with the braid binding by pressing the braid in half lengthwise and fitting over the cut fabric edges (leave about 1.5 cm (⅝″) extra at end of slit). Baste on through all layers, turning braid ends to the inside together with

the triangle created by clipping into the corners. Topstitch close to edge. For the sleeve slit, cut along marked line. Place the bias strip right side to wrong side with 0.5 cm (¼″) seam allowance at lower edge, tailing off to be as narrow as possible at upper end. Stitch, press seam toward slit, turn in seam allowance on other side, and stitch down over the first stitching line. At slit end, stitch the strip together diagonally, right sides facing, to prevent it from turning to the outside.

Gather sleeve at cuff to 19.5 cm (7¾″) for smaller size or 20.5 cm (8⅛″) for larger size. With right side to wrong side, stitch the braid cuff to sleeve, close to edge, folding seam allowance to inside.

Set in the sleeve, wrong sides facing, and trim seam allowance down to 0.5 cm (¼″). Press under one end of the binding, place other end onto the side seam, bind all around armhole, finishing with the pressed-under end. Baste through all layers and stitch close to edge. (Turn sleeve to inside to make stitching easier.)

For the belt, add 3 cm (1¼″) at front edges. Finish cut edges and press to inside. On each side, knot in loop of elastic 6 cm (2½″) long, passing one through toggle. Finally, sew press studs or snaps onto cuffs.

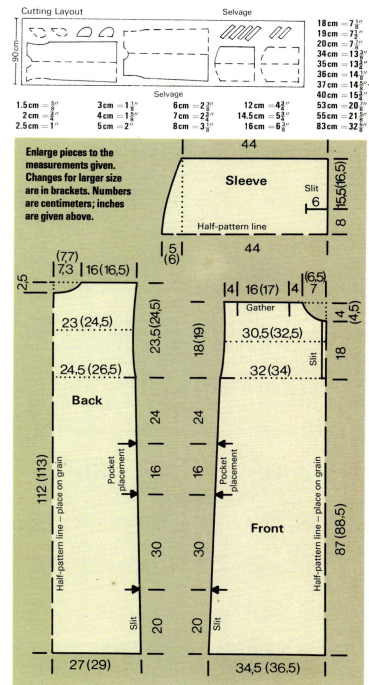

Cutting Layout

Selvage

Selvage

1.5 cm = ⅝″	3 cm = 1⅛″	6 cm = 2⅜″	12 cm = 4¾″	18 cm = 7⅛″
2 cm = ¾″	4 cm = 1⅝″	7 cm = 2¾″	14.5 cm = 5¾″	19 cm = 7½″
2.5 cm = 1″	5 cm = 2″	8 cm = 3⅛″	16 cm = 6⅜″	20 cm = 7⅞″
				34 cm = 13⅜″
				35 cm = 13¾″
				36 cm = 14⅛″
				37 cm = 14½″
				40 cm = 15¾″
				53 cm = 20⅞″
				55 cm = 21⅝″
				83 cm = 32⅝″

Enlarge pieces to the measurements given. Changes for larger size are in brackets. Numbers are centimeters; inches are given above.

Sleeve
Slit
6
15,5 (16,5)
8
44
Half-pattern line
44

Back
(7,7) 7,3 16 (16,5)
2,5
5 (6)
23 (24,5)
24,5 (26,5)
23,5 (24,5)
24
16
30
20
Slit
112 (113)
Half-pattern line – place on grain
27 (29)

Front
(6,5) 7
4 16 (17) 4
Gather
30,5 (32,5)
32 (34)
Slit
18
24
16
30
20
Slit
18 (19)
4 (4,5)
87 (88,5)
Half-pattern line – place on grain
34,5 (36,5)
Pocket placement

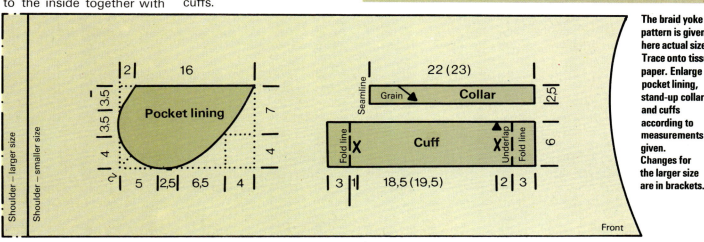

Pocket lining
2 16
3,5 3,5
4
2
5 2,5 6,5 4
7
4
Shoulder – larger size
Shoulder – smaller size

Collar
Seamline
Grain
22 (23)
2,5

Cuff
Fold line
X
18,5 (19,5)
X Underlap
Fold line
3 1
2 3
6

Front

The braid yoke pattern is given here actual size. Trace onto tissue paper. Enlarge pocket lining, stand-up collar and cuffs according to measurements given. Changes for the larger size are in brackets.

Lengths to which you can go

Our versatile pattern gives you two skirts in two lengths for those long summer days.

Size: Waist 63.5 cm—72.5 cm (25"—28½"). The width of the skirt is the same for all sizes. The waist is adjusted to fit your measurements by gathering.

Materials Required:
Short skirt: Cotton fabric: 2.55 m (2¾ yds), 90 cm (36") wide. Long skirt: Cotton fabric: 3.50 m (3⅞ yds), 90 cm (36") wide.

Cutting out: Cut the skirt pattern to the measurements given on the diagram on the right. Before cutting out, check length and width.

Short skirt: Cut out the pieces in single fabric. The pattern shows the half-pattern line at center front and back. Add 2 cm (¾") seam allowance at side seams, 3 cm (1¼") at the hem, and 1 cm (⅜") at the waist.

Long skirt: Cut out the pieces in single fabric. The pattern shows the half-pattern line at center front and back. Add 2 cm (¾") seam allowance at side seams, 3 cm (1¼") at the hem and 1 cm (⅜") at the waist.

Ruffle: Cut 4 strips, each measuring 33 cm (13") wide and 76 cm (30") long, plus 3 cm (1¼") seam allowance at the upper edge and 2 cm (¾") for the hem.

Both styles: Cut out the waistbands in one with the tie ends. (These strips are for a waist measurement of 68 cm (26¾"), ie. 35 cm (13¾") at the front of the skirt and 33 cm (13") at the back. The front of the skirt is a little wider than the back so that the sides can overlap. For a different waist measurement, alter

the length of the waistbands accordingly).
For the front, cut 2 strips each 1 m (39½") long and 6 cm (2½") wide, and 1 strip 35 cm (13¾") long and 6 cm (2½") wide. The strip for the skirt back is cut in one piece, 90 cm (35½") long and only 4 cm (1½") wide so that it will be covered by the front band.

Sewing: Both styles: Finish all cut edges other than at the waist. Join the side seams from the hem to the slit mark. Baste the seam allowance flat along the slit. Press the whole length of the seam. Pull out the basting threads, then stitch around the slit, first close to the edge, then again 1.5 cm (⅝") from the edge.
For a waist measurement of 68 cm (26¾"), gather the front of the skirt to 35 cm (13¾"), the back to 33 cm (13"). The waistband with its tie ends is sewn to the skirt as follows: stitch the 35 cm (13¾") strip in between the two 1 m (39½") long strips. Then stitch one long side of the 35 cm (13¾") strip only to the skirt front, right sides facing. Press the seam toward the band. Then press the seam allowance to the inside all around, press the whole strip in half lengthwise and baste the edges together. Then stitch close to the edge all around. For the skirt back, stitch the center 33 cm (13") of the 90 cm (35½") strip to the skirt, right sides facing. Press the seam toward the band as before. Press the seam allowances to the inside all

▲ **The long summer skirt is made up in a romantic flowered cotton. It has a deep ruffle at the lower edge.**

around. Press the whole strip in half lengthwise and baste the edges together. Stitch close to the edge all around.

Short skirt: Turn under the hem, then stitch close to the edge and again 5 cm (2") from the edge of the hem.

Long skirt: Join the 4 ruffle strips into a circle. Turn

under the hem twice by 1 cm (⅜"). Finish the upper edge. Then turn the seam allowance to the inside and gather the whole ruffle with a 2 cm (¾") head to 180 cm (70¾"). Then stitch the ruffle to the skirt along the marked line. Take care that the 4 joining seams on the ruffle lie flat.

The short version of the skirt is in a striped cotton. It is gathered at the waist and has side slits with ties at front and back.

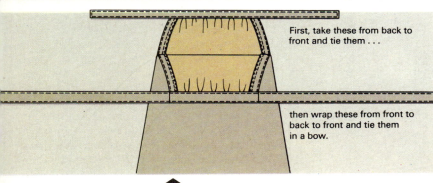

First, take these from back to front and tie them . . .

then wrap these from front to back to front and tie them in a bow.

This diagram shows the bands at the top of the skirt and how to tie them.

Enlarge the pattern pieces to their correct size from this diagram.

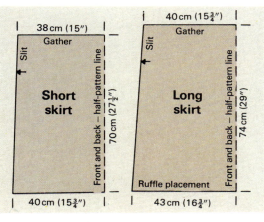

Short skirt

38 cm (15")
Gather
Slit
Front and back – half-pattern line
70 cm (27½")
40 cm (15¾")

Long skirt

40 cm (15¾")
Gather
Slit
Front and back – half-pattern line
74 cm (29")
Ruffle placement
43 cm (16¾")

Bring out the gypsy in you

Size: To fit waist sizes 68 cm–72.5 cm (26½″–28½″).
Materials Required: Cotton fabric:
1st tier: 0.60 m (⅝ yd), 90 cm (36″) wide.
2nd tier: 1.10 m (1¼ yds), 90 cm (36″) wide.
3rd tier: 1.20 m (1⅜ yds), 90 cm (36″) wide.
4th tier: 1.65 m (1⅞ yds), 90 cm (36″) wide or 0.90 m (1 yd), 140 cm (54″) wide.
5th tier: 1.70 m (1⅞ yds), 90 cm (36″) wide.
Elastic: 4 cm (1½″) wide by waist measurement.

Enlarging the pattern

Draw the pattern pieces onto paper according to the measurements given, beginning with the center line and adding the dotted lines at right angles as a guide. Draw in the curved lines as indicated. Add 1 cm (⅜″) seam allowance. Choose pattern piece for 4th tier according to fabric width.

Cutting out

1st tier: The broken line marks the center of the pattern piece. Cut out the whole piece twice on single fabric. Waistband: Cut 2 strips each 8 cm (3″) wide and 48 cm (19″) long plus 1 cm (⅜″) seam allowance. 2nd tier: This tier has a center seam at front and back. Cut out 4 times in single fabric. 3rd tier: As 2nd tier. 4th tier: An added seam is required to obtain the width. For 140 cm (54″) wide fabric, make the seam as indicated on diagram 4A. For 90 cm (36″) wide fabric, place the seam nearer the center (diagram 4B). Cut out the center section twice on the fold, the side sections 4 times on single fabric. 5th tier: Make an additional seam here, too. Cut out the center section on the fold, the side sections 4 times on single fabric.

Sewing

Join the center seams of the 2nd and 3rd tiers and the seams within the 4th and 5th tiers. Finish the seam allowances. Now gather the 2nd tier to the lower width of the 1st tier. Gather the other tiers in the same way. Stitch the tiers together and press the seams upward. Join the side seams. Turn under the hem twice and stitch. Top-stitch around the bottom of the other tiers. Stitch the 2 waistband sections into one long strip, then join to a circle. Stitch one long edge to the skirt, right sides facing, and turn. Fold under the seam allowance on the other edge and stitch along the seamline from the right side, leaving a small opening for the elastic. Insert the elastic into the waistband, draw it up to the required waist measurement and join the ends firmly. Sew up the opening by hand.

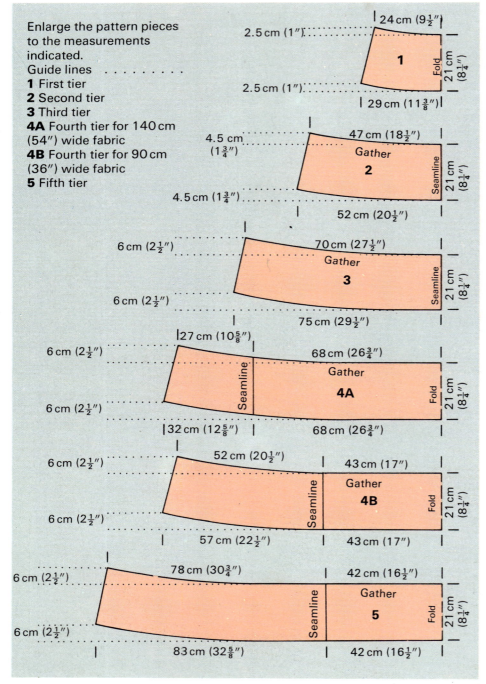

Enlarge the pattern pieces to the measurements indicated.
Guide lines . . . .
1 First tier
2 Second tier
3 Third tier
4A Fourth tier for 140 cm (54″) wide fabric
4B Fourth tier for 90 cm (36″) wide fabric
5 Fifth tier

Our easy-to-wear skirt is made of five tiers in an assortment of cotton prints on a blue background. As a variation, use the same print in different colors, or mix plain with patterns.

Style 1

Fireside fantasies

Dream away the long winter evenings in a romantic flowered skirt. It's cut very full to make the most of a beautiful fabric. One style has a ruffle, the other is plain. Both have set-in pockets.

Style 2

Style 1:
A delightfully old-fashioned print is used for this full, gathered skirt. Simple and quick to make, it has four panels, set-in pockets at the side seams, and is fastened with a back zipper. This style has a wide ruffle with a stand-up head. The long tie belt is optional.

Style 2:
This skirt is in a dramatic print of bright flowers on a dark background. It is made from the same pattern as Style 1, but without a ruffle. Wear it with blouses or pullovers and wear matching woollen tights for a fashionable co-ordinated look.

Size: The gathered skirts can be made for any size. The only measurements you require are waist measurement and length of skirt. To work out skirt width, multiply waist measurement by 3. Waist = 72 cm ($28\frac{1}{3}''$) multiplied by 3 = 216 cm (85″). For a fabric width of 90 cm (36″), you will require 4 panels, so 216 cm (85″) divided by 4 panels = 54 cm ($21\frac{1}{4}''$) for each panel. However, when determining the width, take into account the quality of the fabric and your own size. With a thicker fabric or for a more slimming outline, it is more appropriate to multiply $2\frac{1}{2}$ times your waist measurement.

Materials Required: Style 1: Fabric: 4.10 m ($4\frac{1}{2}$ yds), 90 cm (36″) wide. Style 2: Fabric: 3 m ($3\frac{1}{4}$ yds), 90 cm (36″) wide. Both: Zipper: 18 cm (7″) long. Skirt hook. Iron-on interfacing for the waistband.

Style 1

Cutting out: Enlarge pattern pieces from diagram. Cut out in single fabric. Cut out skirt panel 4 times with 1 cm ($\frac{3}{8}''$) seam allowance at waist and at ruffle placement line and 2 cm ($\frac{3}{4}''$) at all side seams. Cut out waistband once each in fabric and interfacing to equal the waist measurement, plus 2 cm ($\frac{3}{4}''$) for underlap, plus 1 cm ($\frac{3}{8}''$) seam allowance all around. Cut out pocket lining 4 times with 1 cm ($\frac{3}{8}''$) seam allowance all around. For the ruffle, multiply the whole skirt width by 3. In this case, 216 cm (85″) x 3 = 648 cm (255″). For a 90 cm (36″) wide fabric, this means cutting out the ruffle section 7 times, plus 1 ruffle section of 32 cm ($12\frac{5}{8}''$) in length. In each case, add 3 cm ($1\frac{1}{8}''$) hem allowance and 1 cm ($\frac{3}{8}''$) elsewhere. For the tie belt (optional), 255 cm ($100\frac{3}{8}''$) long by 5 cm (2″) wide, cut one strip 170 cm ($66\frac{7}{8}''$) long and one strip 85 cm ($33\frac{1}{2}''$) long, each 10 cm (4″) wide plus 1 cm ($\frac{3}{8}''$) seam allowance all around.

Sewing: Finish the edges of the skirt sections other than at waist edge. Finish the straight edge of pocket lining. Join side seams above and below the pocket slit. With right sides facing, stitch pocket linings to skirt parts, exactly within slit marks (see Illustrated Sewing 16). Press front pocket lining toward the skirt front and stitch close to edge along turned-back edge. Press the other pocket lining toward skirt front and pin pocket parts together, right sides facing. Stitch and finish seams together.

Join center seams, working up to zipper opening only at back. Gather waist edge to waist measurement. (Do not work with one long thread which is inclined to break; use several shorter ones and work in sections.) Try on the skirt and if it seems too full, take in some of the width at center back and front.

Sew in the zipper so that it is covered. Apply interfacing to waistband and stitch to skirt with underlap, catching in loops for hanging up at the sides. The ruffle is stitched to the skirt with a 3 cm ($1\frac{1}{8}''$) head. (If you have altered the skirt width, the width of the ruffle must be altered accordingly.) Finish the edges of the separate sections at short ends and join to a circle. Finish long sides. Press down 1 cm ($\frac{3}{8}''$) seam allowance at upper edge and stitch down. Press under the hem allowance and stitch. At upper edge, gather ruffle to skirt width (here too, work with several gathering threads). Stitch ruffle to skirt along placement line, wrong side to right side. Draw out gathering threads. Finally, sew hook and eye to waistband. For the tie band, press under seam allowance all around, fold in half lengthwise, and stitch together close to edge.

Style 2

Work as for Style 1, but without ruffle. Instead, add a 4 cm ($1\frac{5}{8}''$) hem allowance, press this to inside, and stitch down. Cut out tie belt in one strip (see cutting layout).

Cutting layouts for fabric width of 90 cm (36″). Top: Style 1. Bottom: Style 2. Tie belts are shown by broken lines.

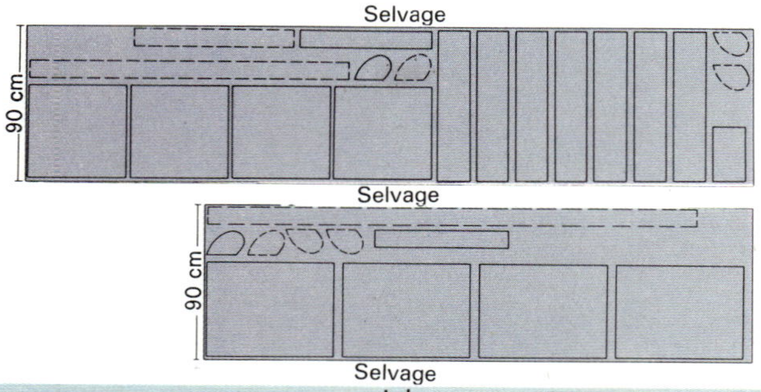

Selvage
90 cm
Selvage
Selvage
90 cm
Selvage

Enlarge the pattern pieces for both skirts from this diagram. Numbers are centimeters, inch equivalents are also given.

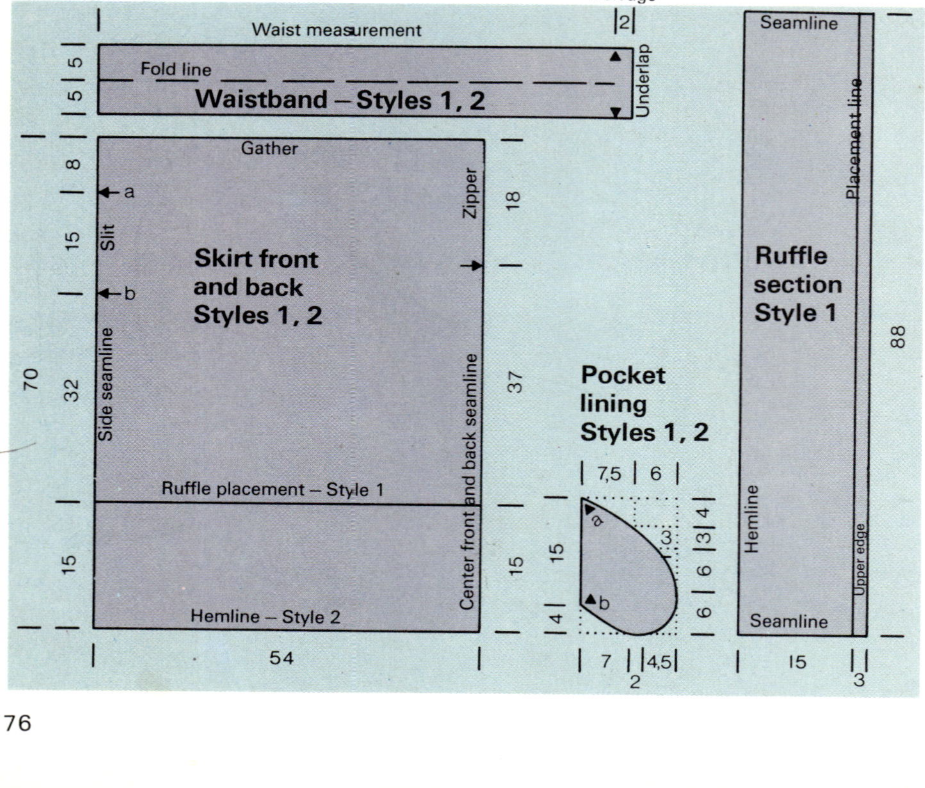

Waist measurement
Fold line
Waistband – Styles 1, 2
Underlap
Gather
Slit
Zipper
Skirt front and back Styles 1, 2
Side seamline
Center front and back seamline
Ruffle placement – Style 1
Hemline – Style 2
Pocket lining Styles 1, 2
Ruffle section Style 1
Seamline
Placement line
Hemline
Upper edge
Seamline
5 5 8 15 32 15 70 18 37 15 54 7,5 6 15 4 7 4,5 2 3 4 6 6 15 3 88

Inch equivalents: 2 cm = $\frac{3}{4}''$; 3 cm = $1\frac{1}{8}''$; 4 cm = $1\frac{5}{8}''$; 4.5 cm = $1\frac{7}{8}''$; 5 cm = 2″; 6 cm = $2\frac{3}{8}''$; 7 cm = $2\frac{3}{4}''$; 7.5 cm = 3″; 8 cm = $3\frac{1}{8}''$; 15 cm = $5\frac{7}{8}''$; 18 cm = $7\frac{1}{8}''$; 32 cm = $12\frac{5}{8}''$; 37 cm = $14\frac{1}{2}''$; 54 cm = $21\frac{1}{4}''$; 70 cm = $27\frac{1}{2}''$; 88 cm = $34\frac{5}{8}''$.

Style 1 skirt is simple and fits snugly over the hips, but is cut with extra fullness below the hip line. The matching fringed triangle can be worn as a shawl or a head scarf.

Matching sets
Country casuals

Here we have three unusual skirt and shawl combinations which can be worn in spring, summer, or autumn, depending on the fabric used. The basic pattern is altered slightly to suit the season and the fabric.

Size: Small: 68 cm (26½") waist, 94 cm (37") hip; Medium: 72.5 cm (28½") waist, 98 cm (38½") hip; Large: 77 cm (30½") waist, 102 cm (40") hip.

Seam allowances: Add 1.5 cm (⅝") to all edges unless otherwise instructed.

STYLE 1

Materials Required: Fabric: 2.20 m (2⅜ yds), 90 cm (36") wide. Fringe: 1.80 m (2 yds), 10 cm (4") deep. Petersham or grosgrain ribbon for waistband interfacing. Skirt hook. Zipper: 20 cm (8") long.

Cutting out: Cut out the skirt pattern 4 times from single fabric, adding 3 cm (1¼") for the hem. Cut out the triangular scarf once. Cut a strip for the waistband 8 cm (3¼") wide to fit your waist measurement plus 3 cm (1¼") for underlap.

Sewing: Join the center back seam up to the zipper. Sew in the zipper. Join center front and side seams. Waistband: Press the strip in half lengthwise. Place the waistband interfacing into the fold line and stitch close to the fold. Finish the raw edge below the interfacing. Stitch the half without interfacing onto the skirt, right sides facing, with a 3 cm (1¼") underlap at center back. Stitch the ends together on the wrong side. Turn to the right side and stitch along the seamline from the right side, catching in loops for hanging up. Top-stitch the waistband and sew on the skirt hook. Turn up the hem and sew.

Triangular scarf: Turn under the seam allowance and stitch. Sew fringe onto the 2 short sides.

STYLE 2

Materials Required: Tartan fabric: 1.30 m (1⅜ yds), 140 cm (54") wide. Petersham or grosgrain ribbon for waistband interfacing. Skirt hook. Zipper: 20 cm (8") long.

Cutting out: The skirt is cut out on the bias. Place the pattern onto the fabric so that the center line lies diagonally on the squares of the tartan pattern. Add 3 cm (1¼") for the hem. Cut out the triangular shawl once, adding 1.5 cm (⅝") for a hem on the long side only.

Waistband: Cut a strip 8 cm (3¼") wide to fit your waist measurement plus 3 cm (1¼") for underlap.

Sewing: Because of the bias cut, stitch the seams with polyester thread and a slightly longer stitch than you normally use. Join the side seams, stitching only up to the base of the zipper on the left side. Sew in the zipper. Waistband: See Style 1. Turn up and sew the hem. Triangular shawl: Draw out threads parallel to the edge on the two short sides until you have a fringe 5 cm (2") long. Then secure the edge of the fabric behind the fringe with a line of stitching. Turn under and stitch the hem on the long side.

STYLE 3

Materials Required: Tweed: 1.20 m (1⅜ yds), 150 cm (60") wide. Fringe: 2.60 m (2⅞ yds), 8 cm (3") deep. Petersham or grosgrain ribbon for waistband interfacing. 5 buttons.

Cutting out: Cut out two fronts up to the band stitching line. Cut out one back piece on the fold. Add 3 cm

$(1\frac{1}{4}")$ for the hem. Cut out the triangular shawl once, adding 1.5 cm $(\frac{5}{8}")$ for a hem on the long side only.

Pocket: Add 5 cm (2") at the upper edge for the facing.

Waistband: Cut a strip 8 cm $(3\frac{1}{4}")$ wide to fit your waist measurement plus 4 cm $(1\frac{1}{2}")$ for underlap.

Sewing: Stitch the front bands to the fronts, right sides facing. Press the seams toward the bands and top-stitch. Fold the bands along the fold line and press. Stitch the side seams and finish the raw edges. Turn up and sew the hem. Fasten the bands at the edge of the hem by hand and top-stitch the front edges.

Waistband: See Style 1. The waistband in this case is open at the front.

Pockets: Finish the seam allowances, then stitch the upper facings to the side seams, right sides facing, and turn. Top-stitch the upper edges and again 4 cm $(1\frac{1}{2}")$ below. Turn under the remaining seam allowances and stitch the pockets to the fronts where indicated on the graph pattern. Work buttonholes onto overlap front band and waistband. Sew on the buttons.

Triangular shawl: Turn under the seam allowance on the long side twice and stitch. Finish the edges on the short sides and stitch on fringe.

Style 3 is a front-buttoned skirt in tweed with large patch pockets and a matching shawl with a fringe trim.

Style 2 is in tartan. The skirt is cut on the bias and has a side zipper. The shawl fringe is made by drawing out threads from the side edges.

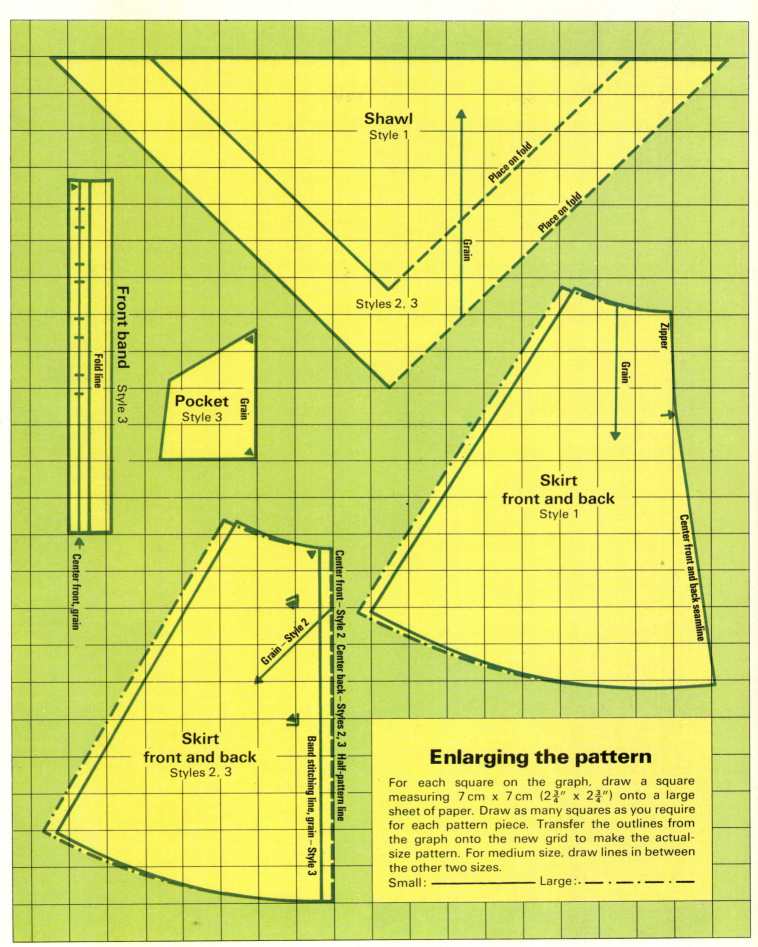

Shawl
Style 1

Place on fold

Grain

Styles 2, 3

Place on fold

Front band

Fold line

Style 3

Center front, grain

Pocket
Style 3

Grain

Zipper

Grain

**Skirt
front and back**
Style 1

Center front and back seamline

Grain – Style 2

Center front – Style 2 Center back – Styles 2, 3 Half-pattern line

Band stitching line, grain – Style 3

**Skirt
front and back**
Styles 2, 3

Enlarging the pattern

For each square on the graph, draw a square measuring 7 cm x 7 cm (2¾" x 2¾") onto a large sheet of paper. Draw as many squares as you require for each pattern piece. Transfer the outlines from the graph onto the new grid to make the actual-size pattern. For medium size, draw lines in between the other two sizes.

Small: —————————— Large:. —·—·—·—·—·

French dressing

An overdress is one of the most versatile fashion garments as it can be accessorized in so many different ways. The style shown here has a narrow cut and plenty of interesting detail to give it a tailored look.

Pocket

9,5 | 8 | 2.5 | 7 | 9,5 | 16 | 2 | 13,5 | 7 | 17,5

Shoulder

Front

26 | 9 | 2 | 7 | 5 | 5 | 8,5 | 23 | 3,5 | 7 | 2 | 2,5 | 10 | 2,5 | 10,5

Pocket slit 16 | 7 | 82 | 83 | 27 | 14 | 108

Hem slit 1,5 | 10,5 | 24,5

Front and back

Center front and back – place on straight of grain

Inch equivalents

1.5 cm = $\frac{5}{8}''$
2 cm = $\frac{3}{4}''$
2.5 cm = $\frac{7}{8}''$
3.5 cm = $1\frac{3}{8}''$
5 cm = $2''$
7 cm = $2\frac{3}{4}''$
8 cm = $3\frac{1}{8}''$
8.5 cm = $3\frac{1}{4}''$
9 cm = $3\frac{1}{2}''$
9.5 cm = $3\frac{3}{4}''$
10 cm = $4''$
10.5 cm = $4\frac{1}{8}''$
13.5 cm = $5\frac{1}{4}''$
14 cm = $5\frac{1}{2}''$
16 cm = $6\frac{1}{4}''$
17.5 cm = $6\frac{7}{8}''$
23 cm = $9''$
24.5 cm = $9\frac{5}{8}''$
26 cm = $10\frac{1}{4}''$
27 cm = $10\frac{5}{8}''$
82 cm = $32\frac{1}{4}''$
83 cm = $32\frac{5}{8}''$
108 cm = $42\frac{3}{8}''$

Size: Bust: 88 cm–92 cm ($34\frac{1}{2}''$–36''). Hips: 94 cm–98 cm (37''–$38\frac{1}{2}''$).

Materials Required:
Wool fabric: 1.75 m ($1\frac{7}{8}$ yds), 150 cm (58'') wide. Iron-on woven interfacing: 0.35 m ($\frac{3}{8}$ yd), 90 cm (36'') wide. 8 buttons. Buttonhole thread for top-stitching.

Note: if using fabric with nap or pattern, you will require additional fabric.

Drawing the pattern:
Enlarge pattern pieces to the measurements given on diagram. Draw the front and back up to shoulder line, then draw a piece for the button band again separately. To finish the neck edge, cut a shaped strip by tracing the outline of front and back neck edge and drawing a second line 3 cm ($1\frac{1}{4}''$) below.

Cutting out: Seam allowances: Add 4 cm ($1\frac{1}{2}''$) for hem, 2 cm ($\frac{3}{4}''$) for sleeve hem, 2 cm ($\frac{3}{4}''$) for side seams tailing off at underarm to 0.5 cm ($\frac{1}{4}''$). No seam allowance is added at front shoulder line; elsewhere add 1 cm ($\frac{3}{8}''$). Cut pattern out in single fabric. The front and back are each cut as one piece.

◀ **This diagram shows the pattern pieces for the overdress. Enlarge them to the given measurements.**

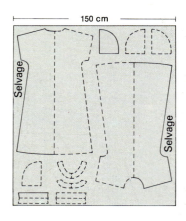

150 cm

Selvage | Selvage

▲ **Cut out in single fabric, following the cutting layout shown above for the most economical placement of the pattern pieces.**

The button band is cut twice with a center fold (see diagram). The pocket is cut 4 times. Cut out shaped strips for neck edge. Cut out and iron on the interfacing for button bands up to 1 cm ($\frac{3}{8}''$) beyond fold.

Sewing: First, join side seams, leaving hem and pocket slits open. Finish seam allowances and press open. Clip into seam allowances at underarms. With right sides facing, stitch pocket pieces to front and back along seamline between arrows (ie. for 16 cm ($6\frac{1}{4}''$)). Press front pocket piece inside and top-stitch opening from right side 0.75 cm ($\frac{1}{4}''$) from edge. Press back pocket part to inside and baste both parts together on dress front. Stitch lower side edge of pocket (7 cm ($2\frac{3}{4}''$)) down along dress side seam. Now stitch pocket shape to front around the edge and again 0.75 cm ($\frac{1}{4}''$) inside the stitching line. Turn under sleeve hem and stitch 0.75 cm ($\frac{1}{4}''$) from edge on right side. Stitch front and back shaped facings at shoulders. Stitch to neck edge and turn. Finish cut edges of front shoulder line.

Stitch short sides of button bands and turn. Stitch one layer of band to back shoulder line. Press seam allowance toward band. Turn in other edge of band and sew along seamline. Top-stitch long sides of bands close to edge and again 0.75 cm ($\frac{1}{4}''$) away; stitch band to front for about 5 cm (2'') up from sleeve hem.

Turn the hem up. Top-stitch hem and side slits in one continuous line 0.75 cm ($\frac{1}{4}''$) from edge. Finally, make buttonholes 2.5 cm (1'') long as shown on diagram. Place first and last ones 2.5 cm (1'') from armhole and neck edge and space the others evenly between. Sew on buttons.

An overdress can be worn loose or belted, teamed up with a blouse or pullover. Our style has short cap sleeves with a button band at the shoulder, side pockets, and a hem slit. All edges are top-stitched with buttonhole thread.

Size: To fit sizes A–C.

Materials Required:

Style 1: Cotton: 3.40 m ($3\frac{3}{4}$ yds), 90 cm (36″) wide. Unfolded bias binding: 1.60 m ($1\frac{3}{4}$ yds), 24 mm (1″) wide. 2 skirt hooks.

Style 2: Corduroy: 3.95 m ($4\frac{3}{8}$ yds), 90 cm (36″) wide. Contrasting fabric for binding edges: 0.60 m ($\frac{5}{8}$ yd), 90 cm (36″) wide. 2 skirt hooks. 1 buckle.

Cutting out: Styles 1 and 2: See cutting layouts. Cut out skirt front and back with 2 cm ($\frac{3}{4}$″) seam allowance at sides, 1 cm ($\frac{3}{8}$″) at waist and underlap, 4 cm ($1\frac{5}{8}$″) for hem. Style 1 is fastened from front to back. Style 2 is fastened in the reverse way. So cut underlap in one with skirt back for Style 1, with skirt front for Style 2.

Style 1: Cut out bodice with 2 cm ($\frac{3}{4}$″) seam allowance on shoulders, 1 cm ($\frac{3}{8}$″) elsewhere. Cut out front and back waistband with 1 cm ($\frac{3}{8}$″) all around; cut the tie band twice with 1 cm ($\frac{3}{8}$″) seam allowance. Cut out pocket 4 times with 1 cm ($\frac{3}{8}$″) all around.

Style 2: Cut out bodice with 2 cm ($\frac{3}{4}$″) seam allowance on shoulders, 1 cm ($\frac{3}{8}$″) at waist, none elsewhere. Cut out front waistband with 1 cm ($\frac{3}{8}$″) seam allowance all around, the back one without seam allowance. Cut out pocket twice without seam allowance. From contrasting fabric, cut 2 cm ($\frac{3}{4}$″) bias strips.

Sewing: Styles 1 and 2: Join shoulder seams; finish.

Style 1: Face neck and armholes with bias binding.

Style 2: Bind neck and armholes with bias strips. Stitch on, right sides facing, with 0.5 cm ($\frac{1}{4}$″) seam allowance. Turn to inside, fold under seam allowance and stitch down from right side along the seamline.

Styles 1 and 2: On bodice, make pleats, placing X onto O.

Style 1: Stitch back waistband to bodice, right sides facing. Stitch and turn tie bands; sew open end. Stitch tie bands to sides, front waistband to bodice.

Style 2: Stitch front waistband to bodice, right sides facing. Bind long sides of back waistband with bias strips as for bodice, then stitch it to bodice seam allowance along seamline, wrong side to right side.

Styles 1 and 2: Join center seams of skirt; finish.

Style 1: Stitch and turn pockets; stitch on.

Style 2: Bind pockets with bias strips and stitch on along bias strip seamline.

Styles 1 and 2: On skirt, make pleats, placing X onto O and stitch down through seam allowance. Join side seams up to slit mark and finish. Press seam allowances toward front on Style 1, toward back on Style 2. Stitch on waistbands, right sides facing, press seam allowances upward. Sew on hooks at sides. Turn up and sew hem.

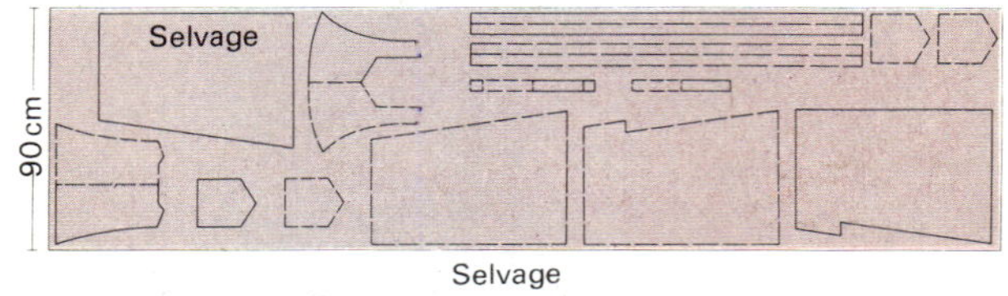

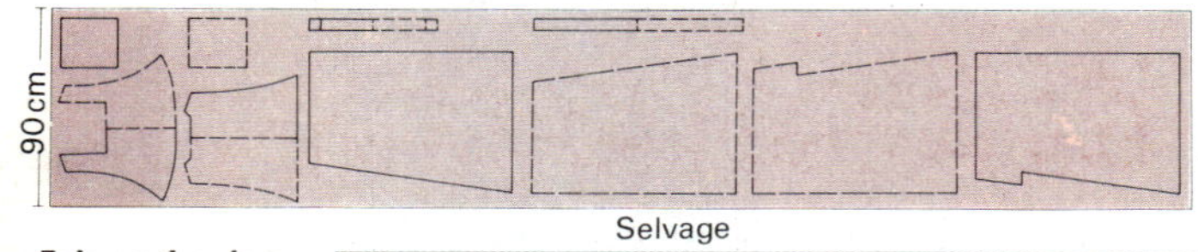

Enlarge the pieces to actual size from this diagram. Measurements are centimeters; inch equivalents are given below.

Inch equivalents:

- 2 cm = $\frac{3}{4}$″
- 2.5 cm = 1″
- 3 cm = $1\frac{1}{8}$″
- 4 cm = $1\frac{5}{8}$″
- 4.3 cm = $1\frac{3}{4}$″
- 4.5 cm = $1\frac{7}{8}$″
- 4.6 cm = $1\frac{7}{8}$″
- 5 cm = 2″
- 5.2 cm = $2\frac{1}{8}$″
- 5.5 cm = $2\frac{1}{4}$″
- 6 cm = $2\frac{3}{8}$″
- 6.5 cm = $2\frac{5}{8}$″
- 7.6 cm = $2\frac{7}{8}$″
- 7.8 cm = 3″
- 8 cm = $3\frac{1}{8}$″
- 8.4 cm = $3\frac{1}{4}$″
- 8.5 cm = $3\frac{1}{4}$″
- 9 cm = $3\frac{1}{2}$″
- 9.5 cm = $3\frac{7}{8}$″
- 10 cm = $3\frac{7}{8}$″
- 10.2 cm = $4\frac{1}{8}$″
- 14.6 cm = $5\frac{5}{8}$″
- 15 cm = $5\frac{7}{8}$″
- 16 cm = $6\frac{1}{4}$″
- 17 cm = $6\frac{3}{4}$″
- 18 cm = $7\frac{1}{8}$″
- 20 cm = $7\frac{7}{8}$″
- 21 cm = $8\frac{1}{4}$″
- 23.5 cm = $9\frac{1}{4}$″
- 37 cm = $14\frac{5}{8}$″
- 50 cm = $19\frac{5}{8}$″
- 55 cm = $21\frac{5}{8}$″
- 70 cm = $27\frac{1}{2}$″

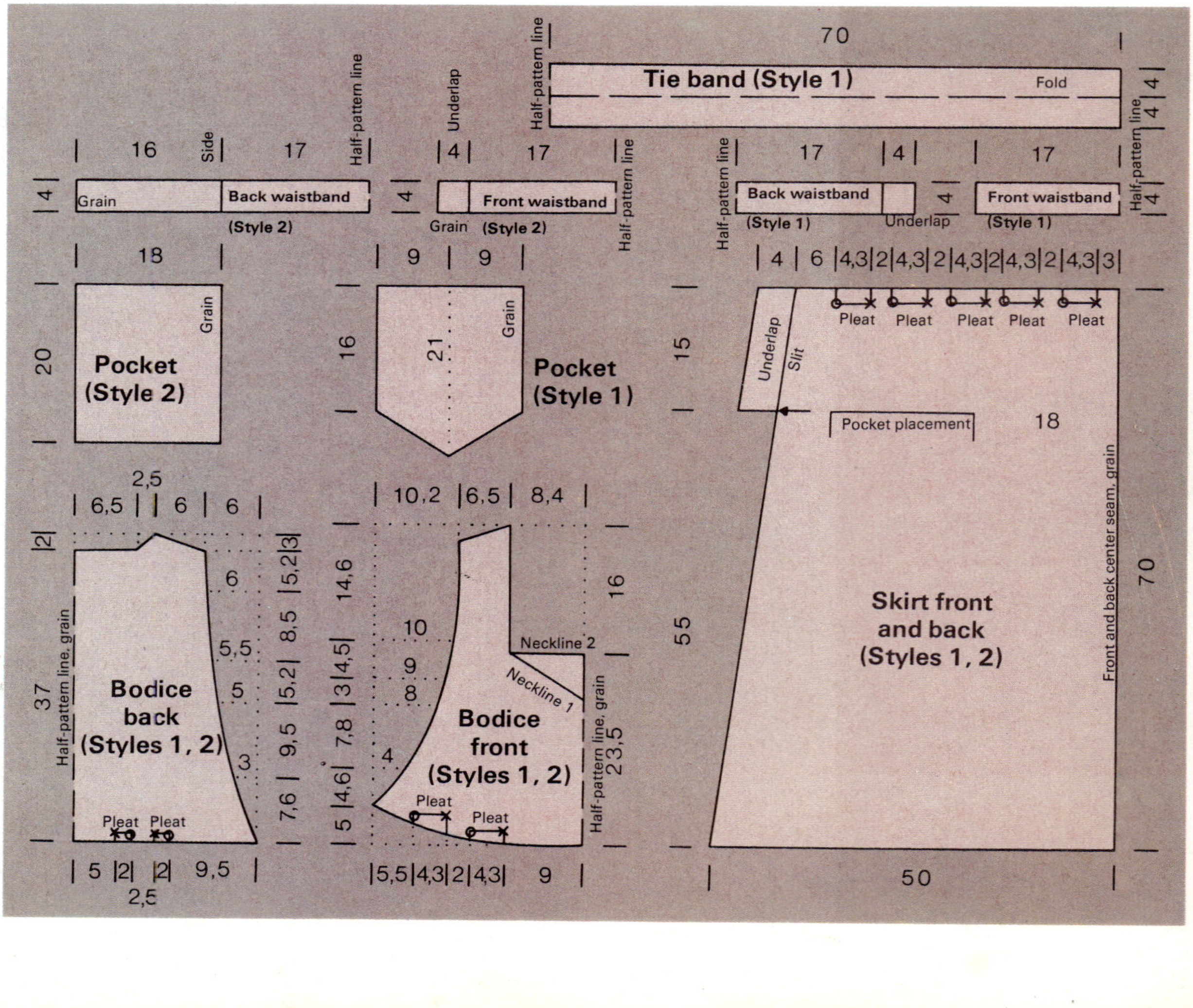

In the pink

Take your pick of these pinafore dresses made from the same pattern. The printed one has a tie band at the waist, the corduroy one has a buckled belt.

Style 1

Style 2

STYLE 1

For indoors or out
Simply stylish

This overdress in a light wool fabric will be one of the most useful garments in your wardrobe. Worn with a pullover, it makes a stylish outfit which is warm enough to wear out-of-doors in the early autumn days. Our pattern is cut wide enough to fit a range of sizes and the simple shape makes it very easy to sew. The sleeves are wide and straight and can be turned back to elbow length. The bias-cut yoke is stitched on over the bodice section; the set-in pockets are simply large rectangles of fabric stitched inside the skirt. The style shown on the left has no fastenings and it has a wide bias band at the neck slit.

84

Size: Bust: 88 cm–96 cm (34½″–37½″), hips: 94 cm–102 cm (37″–40″).
Materials Required: (for both styles) Light woollen fabric: 3.80 m (4⅛ yds), 115 cm (44″) wide. Iron-on non-woven interfacing: remnant for band (Style 1) or for tab (Style 2). 1 button (Style 2).

FOR ALL STYLES

Draw the pattern pieces, following the measurements given on the diagram overleaf.

Seam allowances: Add 3 cm (1¼″) for sleeve and skirt hems, 2 cm (¾″) for side seams, and 1 cm (⅜″) on all other edges.

STYLE 1

Cutting out: See cutting layout.
Sewing: Mark yoke line on back and front pieces with basting thread. Stitch shoulder seams, wrong sides facing, and press open. Press seam allowances of long edges of yoke to wrong side. Pin right side of yoke to wrong side of front and back pieces and stitch around neck edge. Allowing 1 cm (⅜″) seam allowance, cut away excess fabric around neck edge and along band stitching line on front. Snip into seam allowance at neck edge. Turn yoke to right side and top-stitch neck edge. Stitch yoke to front and back along marked lines; baste through all layers around armhole and along band line.

Iron interfacing to each band piece to 1 cm (⅜″) beyond fold line and at lower corners of front opening to prevent tearing. Place bands, right sides facing, and stitch together along the fold line up from lower edge for 8 cm (3″). Stitch each band along the neck curve, right sides facing, and turn. Press in half lengthwise. Stitch interfaced side of bands to front opening along long edge, right sides facing. Clip fabric diagonally at corners and press seams toward band. Stitch narrow edge of band across bottom. Finish remaining raw edges. Top-stitch band 0.5 cm (¼″) from seamline, stitching through other half of bands on wrong side.

Stitch sleeves to back and front from side seam to side seam, matching points **c, d** and **a**. Clip into fabric at corners. Join side seams: leave 12 cm (4¾″) slits open at hem, stitch from here to next arrow, leave an 18 cm (7⅛″) opening, stitch next

STYLE 2
On this version of the overdress, the front slit is held together by a buttoned tab.

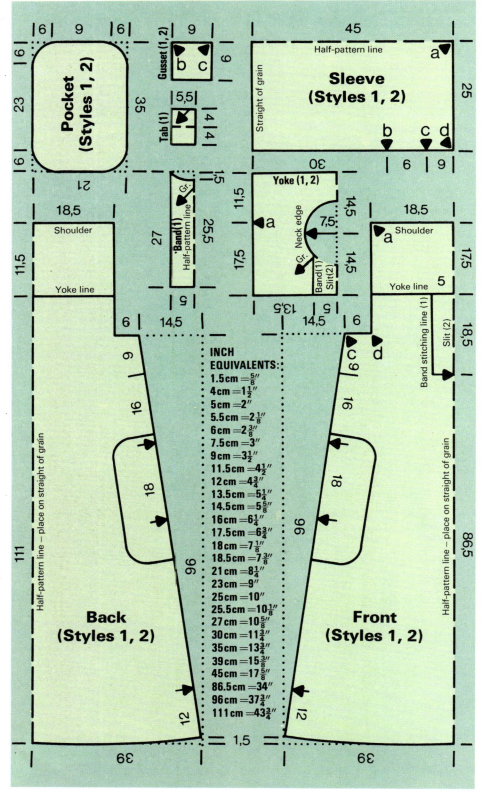

16cm (6¼″), and leave last 9cm (3½″) open for gusset. Press seam open and finish seam allowance. Stitch sleeve from hem to **b**; turn hem under twice and stitch. Set in gusset, matching points **b** and **c**; stitch one side and fasten off before beginning next side. Top-stitch yoke at sleeve seam. Top-stitch side seams all around pocket opening. Finish raw edges of pocket. Baste it under opening in side seam and stitch to skirt back and front along marked lines. Turn the skirt hem under twice; sew in place. Turn in side seam allowance along skirt slit; sew in place.

STYLE 2

Cutting out: See cutting layout. Cut a facing strip for front slit 7cm (2¾″) wide and 18.5cm (7⅜″) long, plus 1cm (⅜″) seam allowance all around.

Sewing: Mark yoke line on back and front with basting thread. Join shoulder seams, wrong sides facing, and press open. Iron interfacing to the tab, stitch, and turn. Top-stitch and work a buttonhole. Pin to right front, 12cm (4¾″) down from the yoke line. Finish facing strip for slit and press under the seam allowance on one short side. Pin strip to front edge, right sides facing, with pressed-under edge at top on the yoke line and stitch a rectangle 0.5cm (¼″) from center line on each side, catching in tab. Press under seam allowances of long edges of yoke. Pin right side of yoke to wrong side of front and back. Stitch around neck edge and front edge down to yoke line. Trim neck edge seam allowance to 1cm (⅜″) and cut slit at center front. Clip diagonally into seam allowance of outer fabric at yoke line. Turn yoke to right side and stitch to front and back at marked line. Baste all layers together at armhole. Turn facing strip to wrong side and top-stitch all around. Work sleeves, pockets, side seams as for Style 1, but turn sleeve hem under 1cm (⅜″) once, then 9cm (3½″) and stitch. Also, note that this style has no side slit. Sew on button.

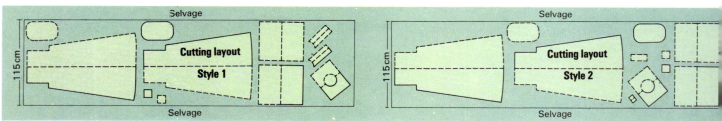

86

Easy winner

Nothing could be simpler to sew than this stunning poncho, and it will make the most of an unusual patterned fabric.

Materials Required: Thick fabric in a suitable pattern: 1.40 m (1½ yds), 140 cm (54″) wide. Fringing: 5.60 m (6⅛ yds).

Cutting out: From the fabric, cut a square 135 cm x 135 cm (52½″ x 52½″), adding 1.5 cm (⅝″) on all edges for hem allowance.

Sewing: Cut the neck slit as on upper diagram and finish edges. Fold the fabric diagonally, right sides facing. To shape shoulders, stitch 2 diagonal lines at either end of neck as in lower diagram. Turn raw neck edges narrowly to inside and stitch from right side. Fold under hem allowance on outer edges of poncho and stitch fringing under hem edge.

We used a gaily-colored woven fabric for the poncho. The fringed border enhances the character of the fabric. ▶

A touch of jean-ius

Here, a pair of flared jeans was used. For the bag, cut off the jeans at crotch level. Make the carrying straps from the upper leg fabric and thread two bamboo sticks through the belt loops to hold the top rigid. From the lower leg parts, you can make a child's skirt on the same principle as the straight skirt.

Transform an old pair of jeans into a skirt and hat. For the skirt, just cut off the legs to the desired length, remove the inside leg seam stitching, and join again as front and back center seams. Work a slit at the back with loop fastenings. The hat is made from the remnants.

Old jeans never die — they can live on forever in different guises. If you have a pair which is worn thin in places, make use of the rest of the fabric to sew a new denim outfit. Here are plenty of ideas for some clever recycling.

The Bermuda shorts are made from a pair of flared jeans which were tight at the knees. The shorts are cut off at knee level and a side slit is made. From the lower legs, you can make the front parts of the bolero. Just buy a piece of suitable fabric for the bolero back and lining.

As a variation, you can make a child's bib skirt. The bib is made from a back leg and pocket and the little skirt is cut from the lower leg parts.

Straight skirt and hat

These are made from a pair of straight-cut jeans.

Skirt: Remove the crotch seam stitching at the front to just below the zipper opening, at the back to the yoke seam. Remove the inside leg seams and pin the front and back legs over one another so that the center seam runs straight. Then try on the skirt. You may find that removing the crotch seam causes wrinkles at the back waist. If this happens, remove the waistband seam to about the side seam and push the surplus width into the waistband. Join the center seams, leaving a 25 cm (10") slit at the lower back, trim off the seam allowance to 1 cm ($\frac{3}{8}$"), and finish cut edges. Stitch the hem. Make 7 loops for the slit fastening and baste under at left edge of slit. Top-stitch slit, catching in the loops. Cover 7 buttons with denim and sew on to correspond to loops.

Hat: $\frac{1}{2}$ of the crown and brim sections are given actual size. Draw the whole of each section onto tissue paper and cut out 4 times each. Iron interfacing onto all the sections, stitch the crown parts together, right sides facing and top-stitch on both sides of the seams. The brim is made double and has a seam at front and back. Stitch along outer edge and turn, then stitch the crown onto the brim, close to the edge. Punch eyelets into crown if desired.

Bag and child's skirt

These are from jeans with tight knees and flared legs.

Bag: You will need 2 bamboo sticks and each 40 cm (16") long and 2 toggles. Cut off the legs at the end of the front crotch seam and sew the jeans together in a slight curve toward the sides. Finish edges. Stitch up the zipper opening. Make straps from the upper legs of the jeans, cutting 2 strips each 6 cm (2½") wide and 50 cm (19½") long. Press 1 cm (⅜") to the inside at long sides, then fold the pressed edges in to the center to make straps 2 cm (¾") wide. Stitch close to pressed edges through all layers. Turn the ends in 4 cm (1½") and stitch them on beside the belt loops at waistband. On the front pockets, fasten a loop and a toggle, stitching the loop under at the pocket edge with the toggle to correspond. Then draw the bamboo sticks through the belt loops.

Child's skirt: You can make this skirt for any age, cutting it as long as the width of the legs will allow. Use one leg for each side of the skirt. Cut off the legs at the required height and remove the inside leg seam stitching and the hem. Leave the outside leg seams joined. Rejoin the inside leg seams to form front and back skirt seams and finish edges. Leave an opening at the back for a 16 cm (6") zipper. Stitch a piece of bias binding to waist, right sides facing, turn to inside and top-stitch the edges. Even up the skirt hem, turn up, and stitch. Make belt loops and stitch on at waist.

Bermuda shorts with bolero, child's bib skirt

These are from jeans with tight knees and flared legs.

Bermuda shorts: Cut off the jeans above the knee and make a slit in the outside leg seam at each side.

Bolero: The pattern pieces are shown on the diagram.

The measurements given will fit an 80 cm (31½") chest. The fronts are cut from the remnants of the legs. Buy a suitable fabric for the back and for the lining. Stitch, turn and top-stitch the flaps. Join front yoke seams, catching in flaps, and top-stitch. Make darts at the back, then join the side seams. Make the lining in the same way. Stitch and turn the bolero and lining and top-stitch close to the edge. Cover buttons with the jeans fabric and stitch over the flaps to fasten them down.

Bib skirt: Make the front and back of skirt as described for the other child's skirt. The bib is made from a back pocket. Cut out with about 3 cm (1") extra at top and sides and 2 cm (¾") at base. For the shoulder straps, check the length with strips of muslin first, then cut 2 strips 6 cm (2½") wide.

The waistband length depends on the waist measurement. Cut 2 strips 6 cm (2½") wide by waist length plus 3 cm (1") underlap. Stitch and turn the straps and punch 3 press stud uppers into each, 3.5 cm (1½") apart. Press 1 cm (⅜") under at top and sides of bib and stitch down. Punch a press stud bottom into each side of bib, 1 cm (⅜") from top. Stitch the waistband along the short sides and the top edge, catching in the bib at the front and the shoulder straps about 3 cm (1") from the center back (with a slight diagonal slant to prevent them slipping off the shoulders). Turn waistband to right side. Stitch one layer of waistband to the skirt, right sides facing. Press seam allowance upward. Turn under the allowance on inner layer and stitch down along the seam from the right side. Punch a press stud into the waistband at back.

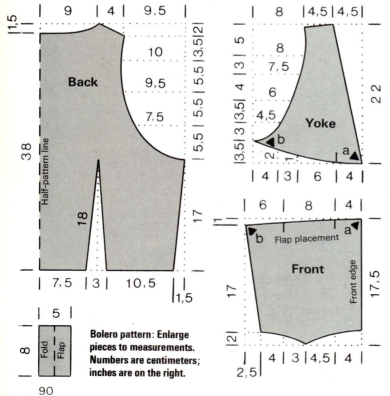

Bolero pattern: Enlarge pieces to measurements. Numbers are centimeters; inches are on the right.

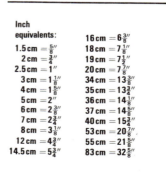

Inch equivalents:		
1.5 cm = $\frac{5}{8}$"	16 cm = 6$\frac{3}{8}$"	
2 cm = $\frac{3}{4}$"	18 cm = 7$\frac{1}{8}$"	
2.5 cm = 1"	19 cm = 7$\frac{1}{2}$"	
3 cm = 1$\frac{1}{8}$"	20 cm = 7$\frac{7}{8}$"	
4 cm = 1$\frac{5}{8}$"	34 cm = 13$\frac{3}{8}$"	
5 cm = 2"	35 cm = 13$\frac{3}{4}$"	
6 cm = 2$\frac{3}{8}$"	36 cm = 14$\frac{1}{8}$"	
7 cm = 2$\frac{3}{4}$"	37 cm = 14$\frac{5}{8}$"	
8 cm = 3$\frac{1}{8}$"	40 cm = 15$\frac{3}{4}$"	
12 cm = 4$\frac{3}{4}$"	53 cm = 20$\frac{7}{8}$"	
14.5 cm = 5$\frac{3}{4}$"	55 cm = 21$\frac{5}{8}$"	
	83 cm = 32$\frac{5}{8}$"	

Sitting pretty

Little girls love to dress up in long skirts. Style 1, shown here, has ruffles, a tie belt, and patch pockets.

Size: Small: 58 cm (23″) waist, 110 cm (43″) height. Medium: 60 cm (23¾″) waist, 122 cm (48″) height. Large: 62 cm (24¼″) waist, 134 cm (53¾″) height.

Materials Required:
Fabric 90 cm (36″) wide for skirt and ruffle. Small: 2.5 m (2¾ yds). Medium: 2.6 m (2⅞ yds). Large: 3 m (3¼ yds). Zipper: 15 cm (6″). Hook and eye.

Seam allowance: Add 1.5 cm (⅝″) to skirt seams and 1 cm (⅜″) to all other edges unless otherwise stated.

STYLE 1

Additional Materials:
Contrasting fabric for ruffle, tie, and pockets: 1.2 m (1⅜ yds). Rickrack: 5.2 m (5¾ yds). Bias binding: 0.7 m (¾ yds).

Cutting out: (from single layer of fabric) Skirt: Cut out skirt piece 4 times, making sure that stripes will meet on center front and back seams. Ruffles: Cut 3 strips each in matching and contrasting fabric 85 cm (33½″) long, 18 cm (7″) wide. Tie belt: Cut 2 strips 80 cm (31½″) long, 6 cm (2½″) wide. Loops: Cut 2 strips 6 cm (2½″) long, 2 cm (¾″) wide. Pocket: Cut 2 on fold.

Sewing: Skirt: Join center front seam. Join center back seam to arrow. Stitch in zipper. Stitch bias binding to waist edge. Fold binding to the wrong side, then top-stitch. Sew on hook and eye. Stitch strips for ruffles together on the short edges to form a circle. Turn under hems of both ruffles twice and baste. Baste rickrack braid under hem fold and top-stitch. Finish top raw edge of ruffles. Gather contrasting ruffle and stitch to skirt, 15 cm (6″) above ruffle stitching line, with right sides facing and ruffle pointing upward. Stitch on bottom ruffle in same way; fold down and press. Pockets: Stitch each pocket together with right sides facing, leaving opening for turning. Turn and sew opening closed. Top-stitch upper edge. Stitch to skirt.

Tie belt: Stitch belt strips to each other at short edges. Fold in half lengthwise, stitch, and turn. Loops: Fold and turn under edges by 0.5 m (¼″). Top-stitch; stitch to side seams.

STYLE 2

Additional Materials:
Matching fabric for waistband and tie: 0.3 m (⅜ yd). Cotton edging: 4.5 m (4⅞ yds), 3 cm (1″) wide.

Cutting out: Skirt: See Style 1. Ruffle: Cut 3 strips 85 cm (33½″) long, 18 cm (7″) wide. Waistband: Cut a strip 64 cm (25¼″) long, 6 cm (2½″) wide. Loops: Cut 4 strips 5 cm (2″) long, 3 cm (1¼″) wide. Tie belt: See Style 1.

Sewing: Skirt: See Style 1. Join waistband to skirt with a 2 cm (¾″) underlap at back. Sew on hook and eye. Loops: Stitch as for Style 1. Sew 2 to the front and 2 to the back. Tie belt: Stitch and turn as for Style 1. Ruffle: Turn under hem twice and baste. Cut edging to fit ruffle hem, press under upper edge; join into a circle and stitch to hem. Baste upper edge of ruffle into regular pleats, and stitch to skirt, right sides facing, as for Style 1. Press under upper edge of cotton edging and stitch to skirt 1 cm (⅜″) above ruffle stitching line.

STYLE 3

Additional Materials:
Matching fabric for pockets: 0.2 m (¼ yd). Bias binding: 4.2 m (4⅝ yds).

Cutting out: Skirt: See Style 1. Ruffle: Cut 3 strips 85 cm (33½″) long, 18 cm (7″) wide, plus 1 cm (⅜″) on short sides, 3 cm (1¼″) at upper edge, and no seam allowance at hem. Pockets: Cut 2 on fold without seam allowances.

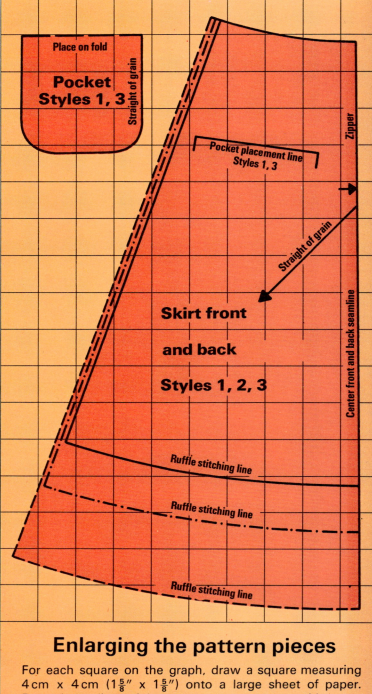

Enlarging the pattern pieces

For each square on the graph, draw a square measuring 4 cm x 4 cm (1⅝″ x 1⅝″) onto a large sheet of paper. Draw the outlines of the pattern onto your new grid.

Small: ——————————
Medium: — ·— ·— ·— ·—
Large: — — — — — —

Sewing: Skirt: See Style 1. Stitch together short ends of ruffle strips to form a circle. Finish upper edge and press seam allowance under. The ruffle is stitched to skirt with a head. Press under edges of bias binding. Stitch to wrong side of ruffle, then fold to right side and top-stitch. Gather ruffle 2 cm (¾″) from top edge. Top-stitch ruffle to skirt. Pockets: Fold in half, wrong sides facing; press. Top-stitch along fold. Bind raw edges with bias binding. Top-stitch to skirt.

For Style 2, we have chosen a tartan fabric. The skirt has a waistband with four loops, a tie belt and a ruffle.

Style 3: Pick a fresh floral cotton. The ruffle and pockets are trimmed with bias binding.

93

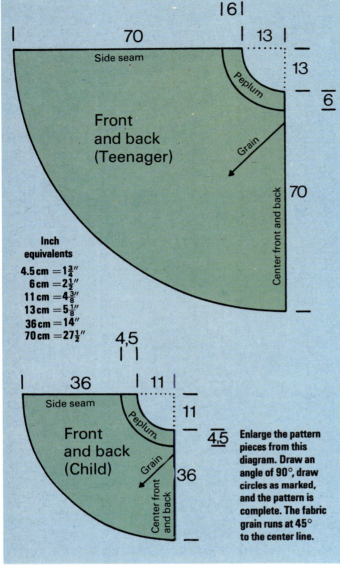

|6|

70

Side seam

13 | 13 |

Peplum

13

|6|

Front
and back
(Teenager)

Grain

70

Center front and back

**Inch
equivalents**
4.5 cm = 1¾"
6 cm = 2½"
11 cm = 4⅜"
13 cm = 5⅛"
36 cm = 14"
70 cm = 27½"

4,5

36 | 11 |

Side seam

Peplum

11

Front
and back
(Child)

4,5

Grain

36

Center front and back

Enlarge the pattern
pieces from this
diagram. Draw an
angle of 90°, draw
circles as marked,
and the pattern is
complete. The fabric
grain runs at 45°
to the center line.

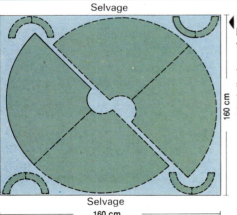

Selvage

Selvage

160 cm

Here is the cutting
layout for the
teenager's skirt.
Cut out the skirt
twice as a
semi-circle and
the peplum 4 times
from single fabric.

The skirt is ▶
gathered at the sides.
On the child's skirt,
shoulder straps are
caught into the
waist seam.

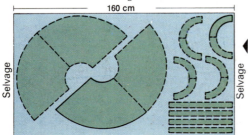

Selvage

160 cm

Selvage

The child's skirt
is also cut out in
single fabric. For
the straps, cut
4 strips in the
length and width
indicated in the
instructions.

Cotton skirt and T-shirt

The young idea

Size: The skirt patterns are given to fit waist sizes 59 cm–68 cm (23¼"–26½") for teenagers and waist sizes 57 cm–59 cm (22½"–23½") for children.

Materials Required:

For Teenager: Cotton or muslin: 2.10 m (2¼ yds), 180 cm (72") wide. White lace edging: 1.30 m (1⅜ yds), about 1 cm (½") wide. Elastic for waist: About 30 cm (12"). Fabric dyes: Pale green and olive green. Thread.

For Child: Cotton or muslin: 1.10 m (1¼ yds), 160 cm (68") wide. White lace edging: 1.10 m (1¼ yds), About 1 cm (½") wide. Elastic for waist: About 20 cm (8"). Fabric dyes: Pale blue and turquoise. Thread.

Note: Buy a white T-shirt and dye this with the skirt in fabric dye for a matching outfit.

Making the pattern

First, wash the fabric, the lace, and the T-shirt. Then, enlarge the pattern to its correct size. To do this, draw an angle of 90°. Measure along 13 cm (5⅛") [child, 11 cm (4⅜")] for the waist; then 19 cm (7½") [child, 15.5 cm (6⅛")] for the peplum.

Draw quarter-circles at these points with a pencil through a loop of string, holding the other end of the string at the point of the angle. Measure the skirt length from the waist and draw a circle.

Cutting out

Both Styles: Check the length of the skirt before cutting out. Following the cutting layout, cut out the skirt twice as semi-circles, with 2 cm (¾") for the hem and 1 cm (⅜") seam allowance elsewhere. Cut out

the peplum 4 times as semi-circles, adding 1 cm (⅜") all around.

For Child: Shoulder straps: Cut 4 strips 45 cm (17¾") long and 4 cm (1½") wide, plus 1 cm (⅜") all around.

Sewing

Both Styles: Join the side seams of the peplum. With right sides facing, stitch the 2 layers together at the outer edge, catching in the lace. Turn and top-stitch. Join the skirt side seams.

For Teenager: Cut 2 pieces of elastic 12 cm (4¾") long, then pin them to the skirt below the marked waistline and stitch across at the ends. Stitch one end 6 cm (2½") from the center front and the other end 10.5 cm (4⅛") from the center back.

For Child: Cut 2 pieces of elastic 6 cm (2½") long. Measure 8 cm (3⅛") from the center front and center back and stitch down the ends of the elastic here, below the waistline. Stitch the shoulder straps together lengthwise and turn. Pin them 6 cm (2½") from the center front and center back, right side to wrong side of skirt.

Both Styles: The finished peplum is now pinned and stitched, right side to wrong side of the skirt. Take care not to catch in the elastic. Turn the peplum to the right side and top-stitch 1.5 cm (⅝") from the top edge through all layers of fabric. Stitch down the ends of the elastic again through all thicknesses. Turn under hem and stitch.

Dyeing

For Teenager: Mix 1 part pale green to ¼ part olive green.

For Child: Mix 1 part turquoise to ¼ part pale blue.

Both Styles: Dye the skirts according to the manufacturer's directions. It is advisable to test the color on a scrap of fabric first.

An idea for summer: dye a T-shirt and skirt in matching colors. Both skirts have attached peplums and elasticized waists. The child's skirt has straps tied into bows at the shoulders.

Patchwork pinafores

These two pretty pinafores have an unusual feature — the bodices are made in simple patchwork.

GINGHAM PINAFORE

Size: 58 cm (23") chest, 57 cm (22½") waist.

Materials Required: Gingham: 1.20 m (1⅜ yds), 90 cm (36") wide in red; 0.10 m (⅛ yd), 90 cm (36") wide each in blue, yellow, pale green, and dark green. Zipper: 20 cm (8") long.

Cutting out: See cutting layout. Cut out skirt twice with 4 cm (1½") hem allowance, 1.5 cm (⅝") seam allowance at the waist, and 2 cm (¾") elsewhere. Cut out front bodice once in one piece (for facing) and once in diagonal strips with a center front seam. Cut the back bodice in the same way but with a center back opening. Add 1.5 cm (⅝") seam allowance on bodice facings and 1 cm (⅜") on diagonal strips. Cut out straps 4 times with 1 cm (⅜") seam allowance all around.

Sewing: Sew the diagonal patchwork strips together to form the bodice quarters and press open seams. Join center front seam, then side seams. Join side seams of plain bodice facing and finish the seam allowance at waist. Stitch the straps, leaving one short side open and turn. Pin to bodice, right sides facing. Pin patchwork and plain bodices together right sides facing, stitch together along top edge, catching in straps; turn. Join center front skirt seam and center back seam up to slit mark and finish raw edges. Turn under hem twice and stitch. Gather at waist to bodice width and stitch the patchwork bodice to skirt, right sides facing. Press seam upward. Press under the seam allowance at center back and stitch in the zipper, stitching it between the patchwork bodice and facing. Baste the bodice facing flat over the waist seam and stitch down through the seam from the right side.

STRIPED PINAFORE

Size: 62 cm (24¼") chest, 59 cm (23¼") waist.

Materials Required: Striped cotton: 1.10 m (1¼ yds), 90 cm (36") wide. Small remnants for patchwork bodice. Bias binding: 3.80 m (4⅛ yds), 2 cm (¾") wide. 10 buttons.

Cutting out: Cut out skirt piece twice with 1.5 cm (⅝") seam allowance at waist, 2 cm (¾") at side seams, but no hem allowance. Cut out the waistband twice with and twice without the underlap and with 1.5 cm (⅝") seam

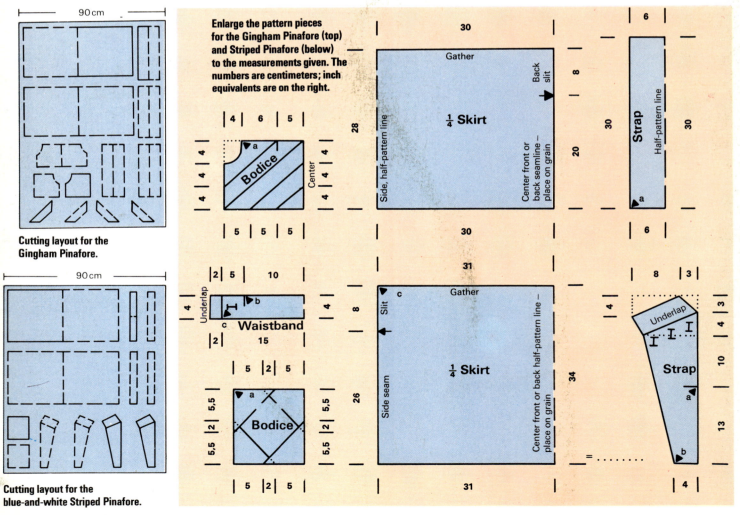

Cutting layout for the Gingham Pinafore.

Cutting layout for the blue-and-white Striped Pinafore.

Enlarge the pattern pieces for the Gingham Pinafore (top) and Striped Pinafore (below) to the measurements given. The numbers are centimeters; inch equivalents are on the right.

allowance all around. Cut out shoulder straps 4 times with 1.5 cm ($\frac{5}{8}$") added at waist, otherwise no seam allowance. Cut out the bodice twice in plain fabric (once for back and once for front facing) with 1.5 cm ($\frac{5}{8}$") seam allowance except at upper edge. Cut out bodice once more in patchwork.

Sewing: Sew up the patchwork bodice. Place the facing onto it wrong sides facing, stitch up the sides and finish them together. Bind the upper edge with bias binding.

Finish the side edges of the back bodice and bind the upper edge.

Now bind the lengthwise edges of the shoulder straps. Then on the front straps, press under the underlap as a seam allowance, leaving the back ones flat. Baste the bodices under the straps where marked, right side to wrong side, and stitch down from the right side along the stitching line of the binding.

Stitch the waistbands together, catching in the bodice parts and leaving the skirt edge open. Turn. Join skirt side seams up to slit mark and finish. Bind edge of hem with bias binding. Gather front and back skirt at waist to 32 cm (12$\frac{5}{8}$") each. Stitch outer layer of the waistband to the skirt, right sides facing. Turn in the seam allowance of the inside layer and sew along the seam by hand.

Finally, make buttonholes at sides and in straps and sew on buttons to correspond.

Inch equivalents:

2 cm = $\frac{3}{4}$"	13 cm = 5$\frac{1}{8}$"
3 cm = 1$\frac{1}{8}$"	15 cm = 6"
4 cm = 1$\frac{5}{8}$"	20 cm = 7$\frac{7}{8}$"
5 cm = 2"	26 cm = 10$\frac{1}{4}$"
5.5 cm = 2$\frac{1}{4}$"	28 cm = 11"
6 cm = 2$\frac{3}{8}$"	30 cm = 11$\frac{3}{4}$"
8 cm = 3$\frac{1}{8}$"	31 cm = 12$\frac{1}{4}$"
10 cm = 4"	34 cm = 13$\frac{3}{8}$"

Simple little smocks

These versatile smocks or coveralls are cut in one piece and can be run up in an evening. Make one for each day of the week in a wide range of easy-care fabrics, not only to keep a small girl clean and tidy, but to make her feel really pretty too.

Size: Small: 110–116 cm (43"–45½") height. Medium: 122–128 cm (48"–50½") height. Large: 134–140 cm (52½"–55") height.

Materials Required: Fabric: 90 cm (36") wide. See individual directions for type of fabric used. Small: 1.5 m (1⅝ yds); Medium: 1.7 m (1⅞ yds); Large: 1.8 m (2 yds). Bias binding tape (Styles 1, 2): 5 m (5½ yds). Extra fabric for bias-cut strips (Styles 3, 5).

For all styles

Enlarge the pattern pieces as instructed on the pattern grid. Check the length and adjust accordingly. One quarter of the pattern is given, so after enlarging the Front/Back piece, cut out another Front/Back piece and tape them together at the shoulders. Fold the fabric in half lengthwise and place the Center Back/Front of the pattern on the fold. You can now cut out the smock in one piece. Cut two ties for front 60 cm (24") long and two for back 45 cm (18") long, all 5 cm (2") wide plus 1 cm (⅜") seam allowance all around.

Style 1

Materials Required: Plastic-coated fabric. Contrasting bias binding tape. Cut out Front/Back and Pocket B without seam allowances. If using non-folded binding, press binding in half lengthwise; turn in raw edges. Place edge of fabric into fold line and stitch all around from right side. Work pocket in same way and stitch in place, adding a stitching line down center to form two half-pockets. With right sides facing, fold ties in half lengthwise. Stitch one long and one short side. Turn and stitch to smock where marked.

Style 2

Materials Required: Towelling. Contrasting bias binding tape.
Work as Style 1, without pocket.

This wrap-around smock is adjustable and allows maximum freedom of movement for an active child.

The smocks can be made up in a variety of plain and printed fabrics. Change the look with different bindings and pockets.

First, tie the back ties in a bow at the front . . .

then tie the front ones in a bow at the back . . .

so that the smock is comfortable and well-fitting.

Style 3

Materials Required: Striped cotton. Bias-cut strips and bias pocket: 0.9 m (1 yd) additional striped cotton.

Cut out Front/Back piece without seam allowance. Cut bias strips 4 cm (1½″) wide for total length of 5 m (5½ yds). Join strips along straight of grain. Press binding in half lengthwise; turn in raw edges. Place edge of fabric into fold of binding and stitch all around. Stitch ties as for Style 1.

Cut out Pocket C on bias with 1 cm (⅜″) seam allowance. Turn under top edge twice and stitch. Turn under seam allowances and stitch in place.

Style 4

Materials Required: Printed cotton. Cut out Front/Back piece with 1 cm (⅜″) seam allowance all around. Turn under seam allowance on all edges twice and stitch. Cut out Pocket A twice with 1.5 cm (⅝″) seam allowance. Turn under all edges twice

and stitch to smock front.

Style 5

Materials Required: Printed cotton. Bias-cut strips: 0.7 m (¾ yd) additional printed cotton.
Work as Style 3, without pocket.

Enlarging the pattern: Draw a grid of 3.5 cm (1⅜″) squares on brown paper or tracing paper. Transfer all outlines and markings to grid and cut out pattern pieces.

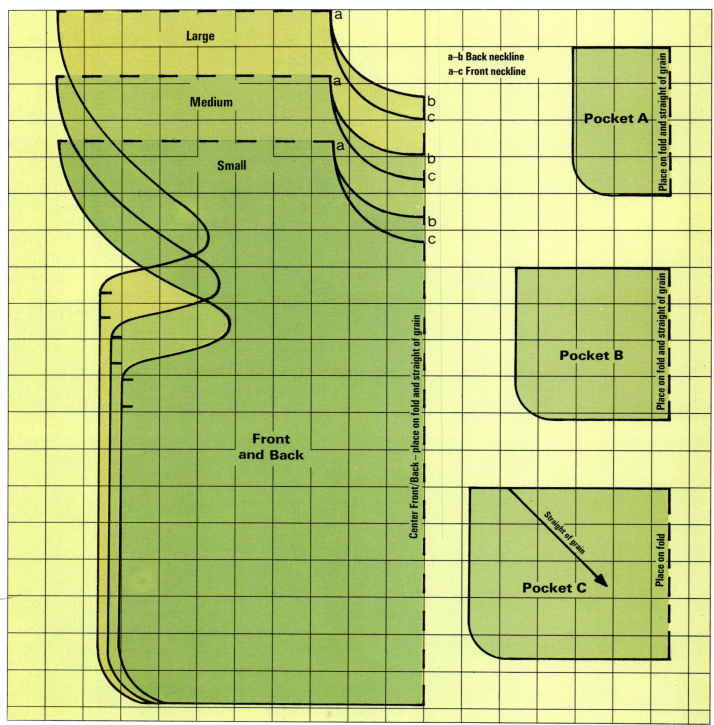

Large

Medium

Small

a–b Back neckline
a–c Front neckline

Pocket A

Place on fold and straight of grain

Pocket B

Place on fold and straight of grain

Front and Back

Center Front/Back – place on fold and straight of grain

Straight of grain

Place on fold

Pocket C

Baby blue

Size: To fit a child 98 cm (38½″) tall.

Materials Required: Fabric: 1.50 m (1⅝ yds), 90 cm (36″) wide. Bias binding: 2.20 m (2⅜ yds), 15 mm (½″) wide.

Cutting out: See cutting layout.

Cut out front and back on fold with 2 cm (¾″) seam allowance at shoulder and side seams, but none elsewhere. If using printed fabric, take care to match pattern on front and back. For the casing at neck edge, cut shaped strips 2 cm (¾″) wide (see broken lines on diagram). Cut out the back strip on the fold, the front strip with center front seam, adding 1 cm (⅜″) all around except at upper edge. For the tie, cut a strip 3 cm (1¼″) wide and 90 cm (36″) long.

Sewing: Join shoulder seams and finish edges. Join shoulder seams of shaped casing strips. Baste them to neck edge, wrong side to right side and edge to edge, turning in the seam allowance at center front. Bind neck edge with bias binding, placing the join on one shoulder seam with one end of binding flat and the other end turned in over it. Turn in the seam allowance on the lower edge of the casing and stitch on close to edge. Bind sleeve hem with bias binding.

Join side seam and finish. Bind hem with bias binding.

Make ties as follows: Press in the seam allowance at narrow ends. Press band in half lengthwise, turn in raw edges so that they meet at center, and stitch together close to edge. Finally draw tie through casing with the aid of a safety pin.

Your little girl will look as pretty as a picture in this sweet nightdress. It has bound edges and a drawstring at the neck.

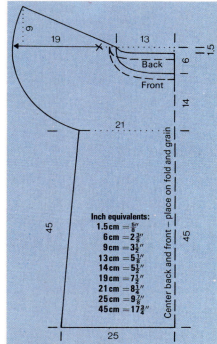

Inch equivalents:
1.5 cm = ⅝″
6 cm = 2⅜″
9 cm = 3½″
13 cm = 5⅛″
14 cm = 5½″
19 cm = 7½″
21 cm = 8¼″
25 cm = 9⅞″
45 cm = 17¾″

The diagram for the nightdress shows front and back pattern pieces, which are alike other than at neck edge. Enlarge the pattern to the measurements given on the pattern above; inch equivalents are also given. From point X (4 cm or 1½″ from neck edge), draw a circular line with a radius of 19 cm (7½″) to find the sleeve length. The broken line at the neck edge indicates the shaped casing strip which is cut separately.

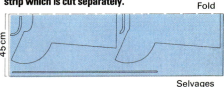

Fold

Selvages

Cutting layout for 90 cm (36″) wide fabric. Cut from double fabric.

Towelling dry

Size: 60 cm–62 cm (23½″–24½″) chest.

Materials Required: Towelling: 2.10 m (2¼ yds), 90 cm (36″) wide. Cotton braid: 5.60 m (6⅛ yds), 3 cm (1¼″) wide.

Cutting out: Enlarge the pattern pieces to actual size from the diagram. Check the length before cutting out. See cutting layout. Seam allowances: add 2 cm (¾″) on front shoulder, side, and sleeve seams; 1 cm (⅜″) on back seams; none elsewhere. Tie bands in cotton braid: 1 strip each for back 125 cm (49″) long, for right front 80 cm (31½″) long, and for left front 58 cm (23″) long.

Sewing: For the tie bands, turn in both ends of back band and one end of each front band to form a point, then secure with zigzag stitching. Join shoulders, sleeves, and sides with flat-fell seams as follows: stitch seam, wrong sides facing and press seam open. Above and below the slit on right side seam, clip into the back seam allowance up to the last stitch. Turn back allowance of slit to wrong side and stitch down with zigzag stitches along cut edge. Fold the wider front seam allowance in half at slit and stitch down with zigzag stitching. Then complete the flat-fell seams as follows: turn in the wider seam allowances around the narrower ones and stitch onto the back, close to edge.

To bind the raw edges with braid, fold braid in half lengthwise and press. Turn in beginning and end 1 cm (⅜″). Fold braid over cut edges of bath robe and baste. Stitch on with zigzag stitching from the right side. Stitch back tie band centrally onto back where marked. Stitch right front band centrally on front, stitch left front band under left front edge.

Stitch and turn the pocket and stitch onto front.

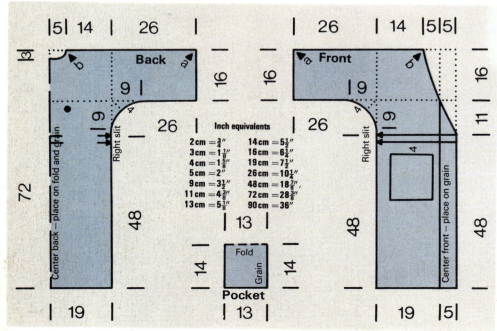

Inch equivalents

2 cm = ¾″	14 cm = 5½″
3 cm = 1⅛″	16 cm = 6¼″
4 cm = 1⅝″	19 cm = 7½″
5 cm = 2″	26 cm = 10¼″
9 cm = 3½″	48 cm = 18⅞″
11 cm = 4¾″	72 cm = 28¾″
13 cm = 5⅛″	90 cm = 36″

Right: Cutting layout. **Left:** Enlarge the pattern pieces to actual size. Numbers are centimeters; see chart for inch equivalents.

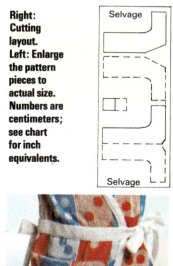

▲ The bath robe is wrapped over and the bands tied at each side.

Children's bathrobes

Towel togas

These bathrobes are such a simple design that even a beginner can make them.

These bathrobes are really roomy so that children will not only find them very comfortable, but will also not outgrow them too quickly.

(1¼") wide for a finished width of 1.5 cm (⅝") and 7 cm (2¾") long, plus seam allowance. Cut the pocket with a seam allowance of 1.5 cm (⅝"). Cut the Front band and tie belt from contrasting fabric, allowing 1 cm (⅜") seam allowance.

SEWING

Join the side seams with flat-fell seams; with the wrong sides of the fabric facing, stitch only as far as the armhole markings. The seam allowances are now on the outside. Snip diagonally into the seam allowances, downward from the top, close to the stitching line. Then, trim the back seam allowance to 0.5 cm (³⁄₁₆"). Turn under the front seam allowance and top-stitch close to the edge. Join the sleeve seams with flat-fell seams; insert at marks. Turn under the hem of the robe and the sleeves twice and top-stitch close to the edge. Work zigzag stitch on one side of the front band and stitch the other side, right sides facing, to the front edge of the garment. Press the seam allowances toward the band. Fold the band in half, then turn in the seam allowance at band hem and slip-stitch together by hand. On the right side, stitch along the seam, catching in the zigzag-stitched edge underneath. Top-stitch all around.
Pocket: Work zigzag stitch all round the edges. Turn under the seam allowance on the top edge, baste in position, and top-stitch once close to the edge, and again 3 cm (1¼") from edge.
Tie belt: Turn in the seam allowances and fold in half lengthwise, wrong sides facing. Top-stitch all around.
Loops: Turn in the seam allowances on the long edges. Fold in half and top-stitch. Turn under the seam allowances on the short edges and stitch to the side seams at the waist.

Size: Two sizes are given: size U, height 122 cm (48") and chest 64 cm (25¼"); size W, height 134 cm (53") and chest 68 cm (26¾").
Fabric Required: 90 cm (36") wide fabric is used.
In 2 colors: Size U, 1.8 m (2 yds) for robe, 1.4 m (1⅝ yds) for trim. Size W, 1.9 m (2⅛ yds) for robe, 1.5, (1¾ yds) for trim.
In 1 color: For both sizes, 2.1 m (2⅜ yds).

CUTTING OUT

Before cutting into the fabric, wash it carefully in case of shrinkage. The Back and Front are cut in one piece. Place the center back along the fold of the fabric so that the front edge lies 1 cm (⅜") inside the fold line. At the front edge, cut along the fold line and around the neck, leaving a 1 cm (⅜") seam allowance. Add 2 cm (¾") on the side and sleeve seams and 6 cm (2⅜") on the hem and lower edge of the sleeve. Cut two belt loops measuring 3 cm

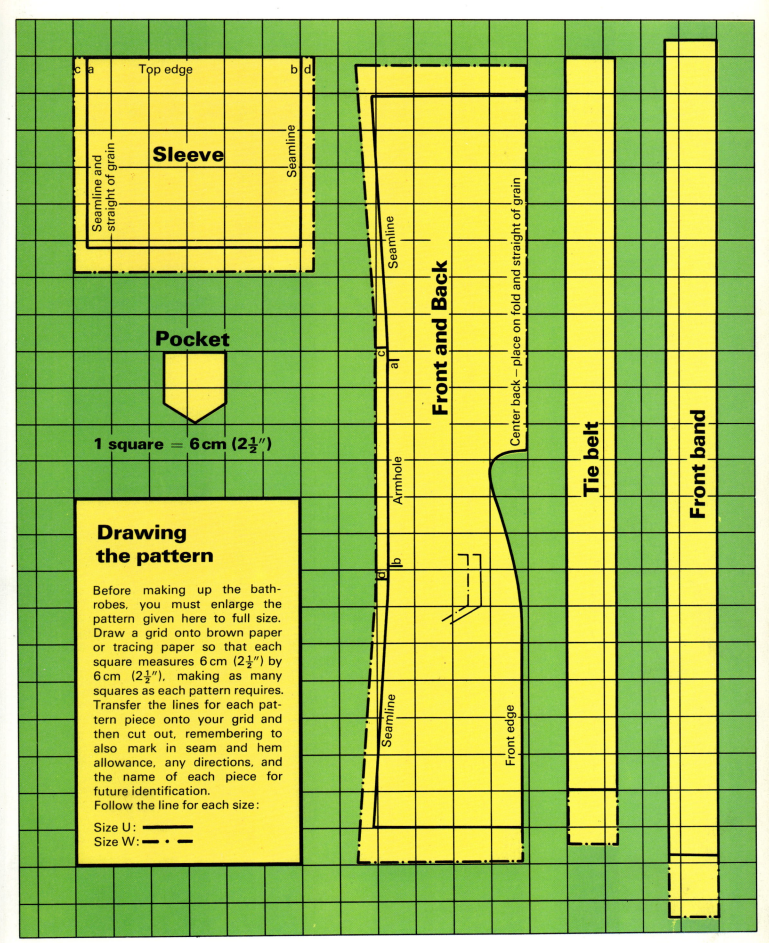

Top edge

c a   b d

Sleeve

Seamline and straight of grain

Seamline

Pocket

1 square = 6 cm (2½″)

Drawing
the pattern

Before making up the bathrobes, you must enlarge the
pattern given here to full size.
Draw a grid onto brown paper
or tracing paper so that each
square measures 6 cm (2½″) by
6 cm (2½″), making as many
squares as each pattern requires.
Transfer the lines for each pattern piece onto your grid and
then cut out, remembering to
also mark in seam and hem
allowance, any directions, and
the name of each piece for
future identification.
Follow the line for each size:

Size U: ——————
Size W: —·—·—·—

Front and Back

Seamline

c
a

Armhole

d b

Seamline

Center back – place on fold and straight of grain

Front edge

Tie belt

Front band

Bathtime is fun time

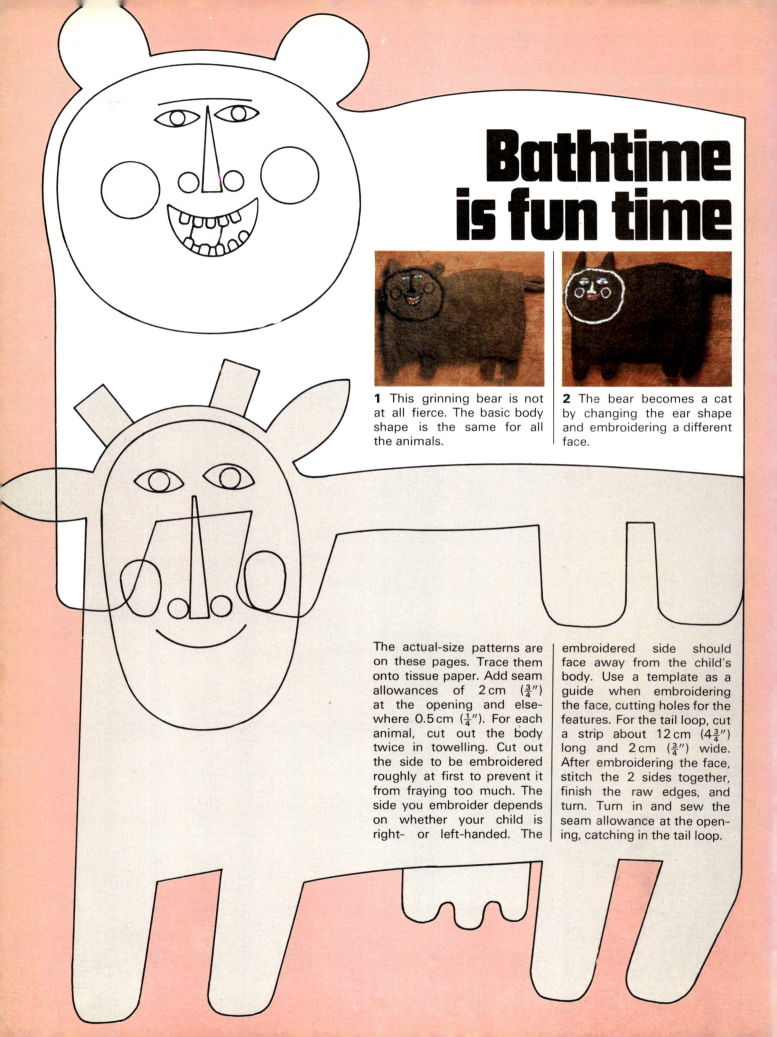

1 This grinning bear is not at all fierce. The basic body shape is the same for all the animals.

2 The bear becomes a cat by changing the ear shape and embroidering a different face.

The actual-size patterns are on these pages. Trace them onto tissue paper. Add seam allowances of 2 cm ($\frac{3}{4}$″) at the opening and elsewhere 0.5 cm ($\frac{1}{4}$″). For each animal, cut out the body twice in towelling. Cut out the side to be embroidered roughly at first to prevent it from fraying too much. The side you embroider depends on whether your child is right- or left-handed. The embroidered side should face away from the child's body. Use a template as a guide when embroidering the face, cutting holes for the features. For the tail loop, cut a strip about 12 cm ($4\frac{3}{4}$″) long and 2 cm ($\frac{3}{4}$″) wide. After embroidering the face, stitch the 2 sides together, finish the raw edges, and turn. Turn in and sew the seam allowance at the opening, catching in the tail loop.

These whimsical animals make washing a great treat, but they can also be stuffed to make a set of lovable play toys.

3 For the cow, use a remnant of black from the cat for horns and pink from our fourth animal.

4 Here's an animal to set you thinking. Could it be a mouse, a pig, or something quite different?

Make a template for the face. Use it to .mark the outlines of the eyes, nose, and mouth with basting thread.

Embroider the features in satin stitch. The head is outlined with a border of satin stitch 0.3 cm ($\frac{1}{8}$") wide.

The jolly lion is made in plain and striped towelling and the mane is made from fringing. The spotted fish, quite at home on dry land, is also made from towelling and the details are applied with zigzag stitch. Enlarge the patterns to actual size from the diagram. The numbers are centimeters; but inch equivalents are also given.

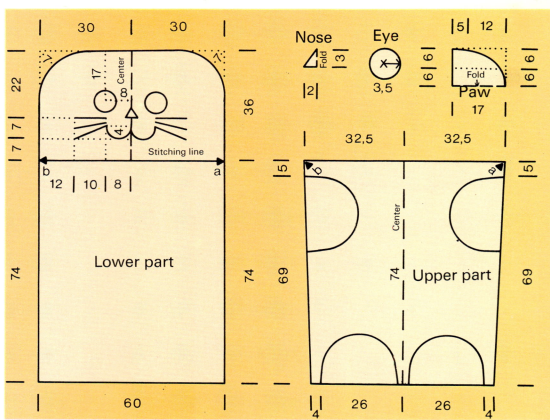

Lower part

Stitching line

Center

b 12 | 10 | 8 | a

60

30 | 30

22 | 7 | 7

74

36

74

Nose
Fold
|3
|2

Eye
3,5

|5| 12
6 | 6
Fold
Paw
17
6 | 6

32,5 | 32,5

Upper part
Center

5

69

74

69

4 | 26 | 26 | 4

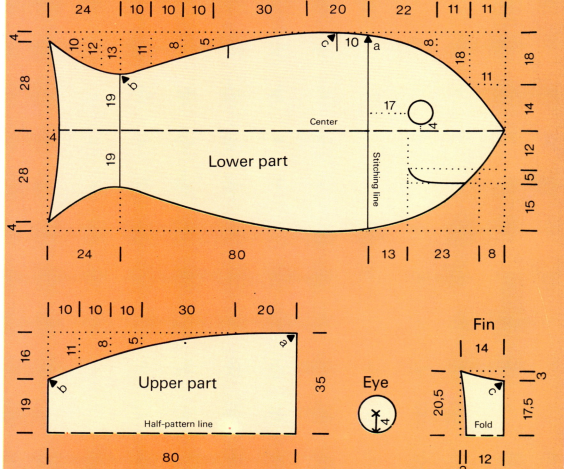

24 | 10 | 10 | 10 | 30 | 20 | 22 | 11 | 11

4
28
28
4

10 | 12 | 13 | 11 | 8 | 5

19
19

b

c | 10 | a

Center

17

4

Stitching line

Lower part

8

18

11

18

14

12

5 | 5

15

24 | 80 | 13 | 23 | 8

10 | 10 | 10 | 30 | 20

16
19

11 | 8 | 5

b

a

Upper part

Half-pattern line

35

80

Eye
4

Fin
14
20,5
17,5 | 3
c
Fold
2 | 12

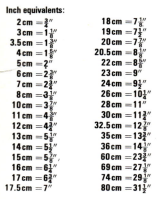

Inch equivalents:

2 cm = 3/4"	18 cm = 7 1/8"
3 cm = 1 1/8"	19 cm = 7 1/2"
3.5 cm = 1 3/8"	20 cm = 7 7/8"
4 cm = 1 5/8"	20.5 cm = 8 1/8"
5 cm = 2"	22 cm = 8 5/8"
6 cm = 2 3/8"	23 cm = 9"
7 cm = 2 3/4"	24 cm = 9 1/2"
8 cm = 3 1/8"	26 cm = 10 1/4"
10 cm = 3 7/8"	28 cm = 11"
11 cm = 4 3/8"	30 cm = 11 3/4"
12 cm = 4 3/4"	32.5 cm = 12 7/8"
13 cm = 5 1/8"	35 cm = 13 3/4"
14 cm = 5 1/2"	36 cm = 14 1/4"
15 cm = 5 7/8"	60 cm = 23 3/4"
16 cm = 6 1/4"	69 cm = 27 1/8"
17 cm = 6 3/4"	74 cm = 29 1/4"
17.5 cm = 7"	80 cm = 31 1/2"

108

Bags of animals

You'll have no trouble persuading the children to have their afternoon rest at the beach if they can snuggle up into one of these animal sleeping bags. They're fun just to play around in, too, and because they are made in towelling, they're ideal for the beach. All the measurements are given on the pattern diagram. This enables you to estimate your fabric requirements and mix and match prints as you wish.

*

LION
Materials Required:
Towelling: See diagram. Batting or wadding: 1.20 m (1⅜ yds), 145 cm (54") wide. Cotton fringing: 2.50 m (2¾ yds).

Cutting out: Cut out lower and upper part twice each with 2 cm (¾") seam allowance all around. Cut out paws 4 times with 2 cm (¾") seam allowance at straight side and none at curved edges. Cut out eye twice and nose once without seam allowance. Cut out following parts in wadding with 2 cm (¾") seam allowance: Lower and upper parts once each, head (above stitching line) once more (so that there is a double layer here).

Sewing: Apply eyes and nose with zigzag stitching. Also mark mouth and whiskers with zigzag stitching. Baste the paws onto the top and zigzag-stitch around the curved edges. Baste the interlining onto each appropriate part. Now stitch just the head part together from point **a** to point **b** and turn to the right side. Clip into seam allowance at end of stitching, then baste the rest of the two parts together, wrong sides facing. Finish raw edges together. Stitch together along head stitch-

ing line. Stitch the upper part together along the opening edge, turn, and top-stitch. Then baste together all around, wrong sides facing, and finish raw edges together. Now stitch lower part to upper part as follows: place top side of upper part on bottom side of lower part. Stitch together around outer edges and turn. Finally stitch on 2 staggered rows of fringing.

FISH
Materials Required:
Towelling: See diagram. Batting or wadding: 1.55 m (1¾ yds), 145 cm (54") wide.

Cutting out: Add 2 cm (¾") seam allowances. Cut lower part once with and once without tail. Cut upper part and fin twice each, the tail once. Cut out eye once without seam allowance. Cut following parts once each in interlining: lower part including tail, fin, upper part, and head once again above stitching line (to make double layer here).

Sewing: Apply eye and mark mouth with zigzag stitching. Baste interlining onto relevant parts. Stitch head together to stitching line and turn. Clip into seam allowance at end of stitching. Then baste rest of 2 lower parts together, wrong sides facing, finishing raw edges together. Stitch along head stitching line. Stitch upper parts together along opening edge and lower edge, stitching on separate tail piece here. Stitch fin together, leaving straight side open. Turn and top-stitch. Baste to lower part where marked, catching it in finally when stitching the 2 parts together. Place top side of upper part on bottom side of lower part, stitch, then turn. Finally stitch through all layers along tail line.

Lots of sewing ideas

Specially designed for baby

Here, and on the following pages are lots of pretty and practical items specially created with baby in mind. They are all easy to sew, economical, and would make wonderful presents for any new mother. In the photograph above, you can see how comfortable our baby looks in his bed lined with a well-padded surround to prevent him from hurting himself. The pillowcase and cover are made of towelling.

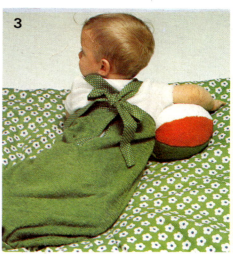

DOLL

Height: 27 cm (10½").
Materials Required:
Towelling. Remnants of yarn and decorative edging. Bias binding. Kapok for stuffing.

Cut out the doll's body twice in towelling and sew together, leaving an opening in the head. Turn and stuff with kapok. Sew up the opening by hand. Embroider eyes and a mouth with satin stitch. Sew a fringe of cotton yarn onto the head for hair. Make the little cap and bind with bias binding. Sew a length on either side for tying a bow. Stuff a little kapok into the back of the cap to make the head round. Place the cap on the head with the hair showing. Sew the cap in place.

Cut out the dress twice on the fold, then stitch the side seams. Sew hem, catching in edging under the hem. Dress the doll and sew shoulder seams.

BALL

Materials Required:
Towelling. Kapok. Cut out the towelling segments 6 times with a 1 cm (⅜") seam allowance. Stitch the segments together, leaving an opening in the center of last seam. Turn, stuff with kapok, sew up opening.

PLAYSUIT

Materials Required: Soft towelling: 40 cm x 104 cm (15¾" x 41"). Dotted cotton: 20 cm (¼ yd), 90 cm (36") wide. Scrap of white cotton. A quarter of the playsuit is given on the graph pattern.

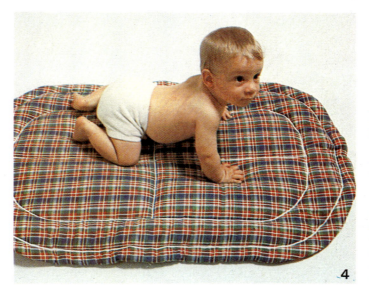

1 It's very important that your baby's toys are soft so that he cannot hurt himself. The little doll and the ball are made of towelling stuffed with kapok and are very huggable.

2 This roomy playsuit gives a baby plenty of kicking room, but is also nice and warm.

3 The shoulder straps, which are sewn to the front, are crossed at the back and tied into a bow.

4 A changing mat is indispensible for baby's comfort and yours. This mat is made of cotton, filled with a layer of batting or wadding and trimmed with braid to hold the layers together.

Trace the piece twice and tape together, adding 1 cm (⅜") seam allowance at the sides. Cut the playsuit in one piece, placing the bottom on the fold.
Stitch the side seams and finish with zigzag stitching.

Cut a 18 cm (7") slit down the center back and bind this and the upper edge with the dotted cotton so that the finished width is 0.5 cm (¼"). At the left and right of the slit, sew two 5 cm (2") loops for the ties. Cut 2 strips of

dotted cotton 6 cm (2½") wide by 65 cm (25½") long plus seam allowance. Fold, stitch, and turn to make ties. Sew at the front 3 cm (1¼") to the left and right of center. These are crossed over at the back, threaded

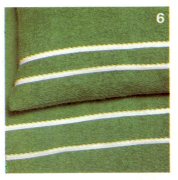

together. Cut out the top and bottom of the mat with a 1 cm ($\frac{3}{8}$″) seam allowance, the interlining without a seam allowance. Tack the interlining to the bottom piece of the mat. Stitch the top and bottom together, right sides facing, then turn to the right side.

Finally, stitch the narrow braid to the top of the mat along the two oval lines marked on the pattern, through all layers. Stitch a cross inside the inner oval.

BIB

Materials Required:
Towelling: 25 cm x 60 cm (10″ x 23$\frac{3}{4}$″). White bias binding: 0.50 m ($\frac{1}{2}$ yd). Decorative braid: 2 m (2$\frac{1}{4}$ yds), 2 cm ($\frac{3}{4}$″) wide. Tape or ribbon for ties: 0.90 m (1 yd).

A quarter of the bib is given. Trace twice and tape together. Cut out on fold with 1 cm ($\frac{3}{8}$″) seam allowance (neck edge has no seam allowance). At center back, cut a slit 10 cm (4″) long; bind slit and neck edge with white bias binding. Finish seam allowances with zigzag stitching, then turn to inside and baste. Bind the outer edges of the bib with braid. Stitch a 22 cm (8$\frac{1}{2}$″) length of tape onto each corner of armhole opening.

DUVET AND PILLOW SET

Sizes: Duvet: 75 cm (29$\frac{1}{2}$″) square. Pillow: 40 cm x 30 cm (15$\frac{3}{4}$″ x 11$\frac{3}{4}$″).
Materials Required: Soft towelling: 1.95 m (2$\frac{1}{8}$ yds), 90 cm (36″) wide. Thick batting or wadding: 2.65 m (2$\frac{7}{8}$ yds), 90 cm (36″) wide. Cotton: 1.80 m (2 yds), 90 cm (36″) wide. Braid: 2.50 m (2$\frac{3}{4}$ yds). Large flat press studs or snaps.
Note: This method of making covers can be adapted to any size by altering the measurements. For the duvet cover, cut

5 A large bib in towelling is very practical and can easily be washed in the washing machine.

6 An idea for baby's bed: Make covers from bright towelling trimmed with white braid.

7 The cot has a padded surround so that baby cannot knock himself against the sides. It consists of three separate cushions fastened to the rails with ties.

8 A night-time sleeping bag for sweet dreams. It is trimmed with a colorful braid border and has a zipper at the front.

9 This is a warm towel with a trimmed hood that you can wrap baby in after his bath.

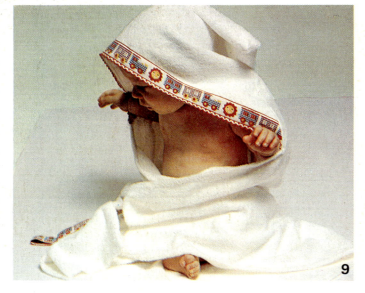

through the loops, and tied in a bow. Finally, cut out the flower motif in dotted cotton, appliqué a circle in the center in white fabric, and stitch to the front of the playsuit with zigzag stitching.

CHANGING MAT

Size: 95 cm x 62 cm (37$\frac{1}{2}$″ x 24$\frac{1}{2}$″).
Materials Required:
Checked cotton fabric: 2 m (2$\frac{1}{4}$ yds), 90 cm (36″) wide. White cotton braid: 5.60 m

(6$\frac{1}{8}$ yds), 0.5 cm ($\frac{1}{4}$″) wide. Batting or wadding for interlining: 0.65 m ($\frac{3}{4}$ yd), 115 cm (45″) wide (pieced if necessary).

A quarter of the mat is given on the graph pattern. Trace 4 times and tape

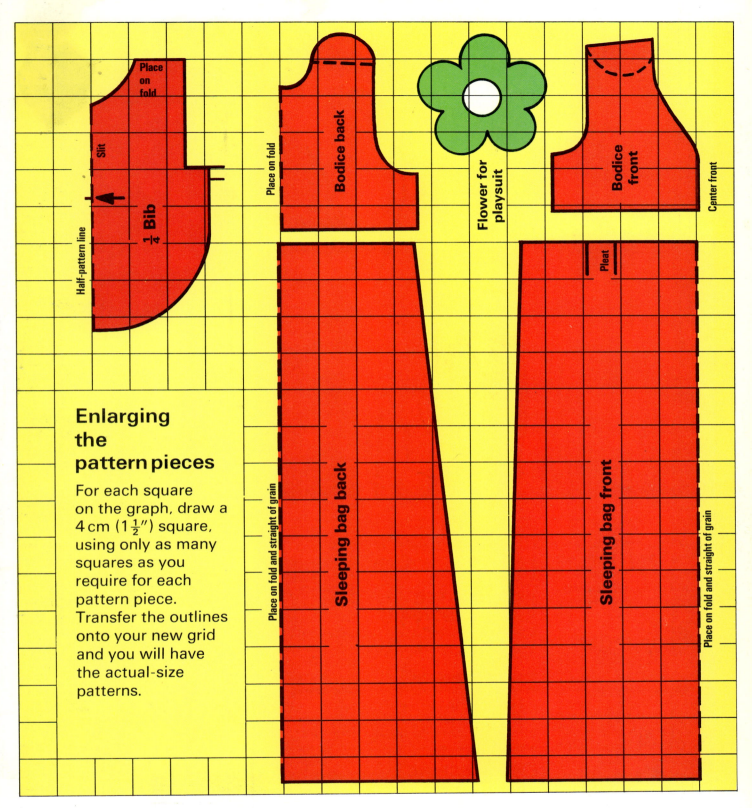

Place on fold

Slit

Half-pattern line

¼ Bib

Place on fold

Bodice back

Flower for playsuit

Bodice front

Center front

Pleat

Place on fold and straight of grain

Sleeping bag back

Sleeping bag front

Place on fold and straight of grain

Enlarging the pattern pieces

For each square on the graph, draw a 4 cm (1½″) square, using only as many squares as you require for each pattern piece. Transfer the outlines onto your new grid and you will have the actual-size patterns.

a piece measuring 75 cm x 160 cm (29½″ x 63″) plus a 1 cm (⅜″) seam allowance on the long sides. Make flat hems 3 cm (1¼″) wide on the two narrow ends.

On one end of the cover, stitch two lines of braid 5 cm (2″) apart and 10 cm

(4″) from the edge.

Fold the fabric, right sides facing, so that the side with the braid measures 75 cm (29½″) and the other 79 cm (31″). Fold the extra 4 cm (1½″) over the other edge (hem over hem) and pin down. Stitch both side

seams and turn the cover to the right side. Sew large flat plastic studs or snaps in between the hems.

For pillow cover, cut a strip 30 cm x 90 cm (12″ x 36″) with a 1 cm (⅜″) seam allowance on the long sides. Make the pillow

cover in the same way as the duvet cover. The braid is sewn on 4 cm (1½″) apart and the same distance from one long seam.

To make the pillow, cut 3 pieces of batting or wadding 40 cm x 30 cm (15¾″ x 11¾″) and overcast the

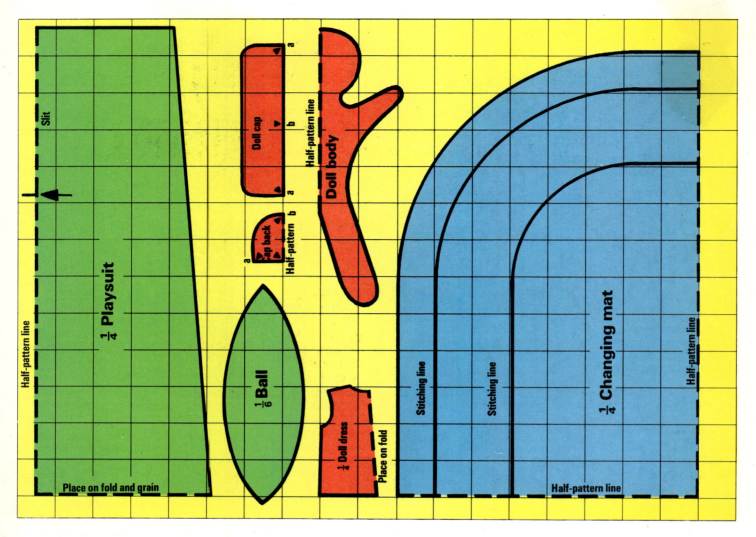

Pattern pieces labels (as shown in diagram):

- Slit
- Half-pattern line
- ¼ Playsuit
- Place on fold and grain
- Doll cap (a, b)
- Cap back (a, b) — Half-pattern
- Half-pattern line
- Doll body
- ⅙ Ball
- ¼ Doll dress — Place on fold
- Stitching line
- Stitching line
- ¼ Changing mat
- Half-pattern line
- Half-pattern line

edges. Make an inner cover for the pillow from the cotton. Insert the pillow in the towelling cover. Make the duvet in the same way.

BED SURROUND

Size: Each panel is 37 cm x 55 cm (14⅝″ x 21⅝″).

Materials Required:
Checked cotton fabric: 1.60 m (1¾ yds), 90 cm (36″) wide. Batting or wadding: 1 m (1⅛ yds), 90 cm (36″) wide. Embroidered white edging: 4.80 m (5¼ yds). White tape or ribbon for ties: 2.40 m (2⅝ yds).
Cut out 2 pieces for each panel with 1 cm (⅜″) seam allowance. Cut the filling without seam allowance. Stitch the panel pieces together with the slightly gathered edging stitched into 2 narrow and 1 long side. Turn and insert the

filling. Fasten 2 pieces of tape 20 cm (8″) long onto each upper corner.

PRINTED PILLOWCASE

(Photographs 2 and 3).
Size: 48 cm x 76 cm (19″ x 30″)

Materials Required:
Printed cotton: 1.10 m (1¾ yds), 90 cm (36″) wide. Work in the same way as the green towelling duvet and pillow covers.

SLEEPING BAG

Materials Required: Soft towelling: 1.20 m (1⅜ yds), 90 cm (36″) wide. Soft lining fabric: Same as for towelling. Children's braid: 0.65 m (¾ yd) long. White bias binding: 2.30 m (2½ yds). Zipper: 55 cm (22″) long.
Cut out the sleeping bag

back and front and the back bodice on the fold. Add 1.5 cm (⅝″) seam allowance only to the side seams and the lower end. Place the wrong side of the pieces onto the lining fabric and cut out in the same way. Towelling and lining are worked as one. Stitch side seams and the bottom seam of the bag. Finish with zigzag stitching.
Then cut a 45 cm (17¾″) slit in the front bag piece and bind with white bias binding. Join the bodice pieces at the side seams. Bind the sleeve, shoulder, and neck edges with bias binding. Place the rounded end of the back shoulder strap over the front shoulder strap, and stitch together along the curve.
Stitch the children's braid to the bodice, and then the bag, folding the front into

pleats where indicated. Finally, stitch in the zipper.

BATH TOWEL WITH HOOD

Size: 95 cm (37½″) square.
Materials Required:
Towelling: 1.60 m (1¾ yds), 115 cm (45″) wide. Children's embroidered braid: 55 cm (22″) long.
Cut out the 95 cm (37½″) square towel with a 1 cm (⅜″) seam allowance all around. Also cut out a right-angled triangle with sides 36 cm, 36 cm, and 50 cm (14″, 14″, and 19½″) long plus a 1 cm (⅜″) seam allowance all around.
Stitch the braid to the longest side of the triangle. Stitch the 2 short sides of the triangle on either side of a corner point of the towel. Turn under the remaining raw edges twice and stitch in place.

Reining champion

Toddlers need a helping hand while they are learning to walk and our baby reins provide a practical solution. Decorate them with bells for fun and add baby's name in colored braid.

Materials Required:
Cotton or canvas fabric: 0.30 m ($\frac{3}{8}$ yd), 140 cm (54″) wide. Belt webbing: 1.25 m (1$\frac{3}{8}$ yds), 3 cm (1$\frac{1}{8}$″) wide and 0.65 m ($\frac{3}{4}$ yd), 4 cm (1$\frac{1}{2}$″) wide. Remnants of soutache braid for the name. 1 spool each of sewing thread and buttonhole twist. 2 buttons. 4 bells. 1 sew-on motif.

Cutting out:
Cut out each pattern strip once, adding 1 cm ($\frac{3}{8}$″) all around for seam allowance. Cut the 3 cm (1$\frac{1}{8}$″) webbing for the shoulder straps and chest band (for measurements, see diagram). Cut the 4 cm (1$\frac{1}{2}$″) wide webbing for the front and back waistband (for measurements, see diagram).

Sewing:
On all strips of fabric, stitch the long sides and turn. Draw the lengths of webbing through the relevant parts. Turn in seam allowance at short ends of strips and sew up by hand, leaving only the sloping ends of the shoulder straps open. Top-stitch the 2 waistbands 0.5 cm ($\frac{1}{4}$″) from edge all around. On front waistband, draw the name lightly in pencil between the 2 shoulder straps. Sew on braid with small hand stitches, knotting each end securely.
Baste, then stitch shoulder straps to front waistband (see dotted lines on diagram), top-stitching edges of straps all around except for sloping ends.
Baste, then stitch chest band to shoulder straps (see dotted lines on diagram), top-stitching all around. Baste ends of shoulder straps, crossed over at back, to back waistband (see dotted lines on diagram). Turn seam allowances to inside and stitch strap ends down.
Work machine buttonholes into the reins and into the front waistband. Sew buttons onto back waistband. Sew the motif onto the chest band and sew bells on either side. Sew the other bells onto the front ends of the shoulder straps. The waistbands are buttoned together at the sides and the reins buttoned on here (see photograph below).

The sturdy reins are made up of straps of various lengths. Four little bells, and the name and motif are pretty decorations.

Inch equivalents:
1 cm = $\frac{3}{8}$″
2 cm = $\frac{3}{4}$″
3 cm = 1$\frac{1}{8}$″
3.5 cm = 1$\frac{3}{8}$″
6.5 cm = 2$\frac{5}{8}$″
7 cm = 2$\frac{3}{4}$″
10.5 cm = 4$\frac{1}{8}$″
11 cm = 4$\frac{3}{8}$″
19 cm = 7$\frac{1}{2}$″
31.5 cm = 12$\frac{1}{8}$″
35.5 cm = 14″
51 cm = 20$\frac{1}{8}$″
117 cm = 46$\frac{1}{8}$″
125 cm = 49$\frac{1}{8}$″

The pattern pieces for the baby reins are given here. Enlarge to the measurements given. The numbers are centimeters (inch equivalents given).

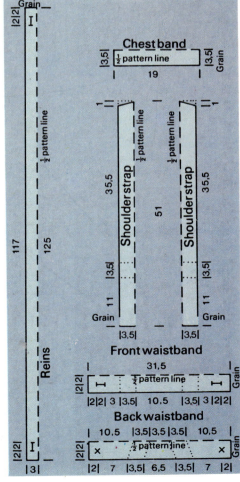

Grain

Chest band
|3,5| $\frac{1}{2}$ pattern line |3,5| Grain
19

Shoulder strap — Shoulder strap
35.5   51   35.5
11 |3,5| 11
Grain   Front waistband   Grain
|3,5| |3,5|

Reins
117 125

Front waistband
31.5
|2|2| $\frac{1}{2}$ pattern line Grain
|2|2| 3 |3,5| 10.5 |3,5| 3 |2|2|

Back waistband
10.5 |3,5|3,5|3,5| 10.5
|2|2| x $\frac{1}{2}$ pattern line x Grain
|3| |2| 7 |3,5| 6,5 |3,5| 7 |2|

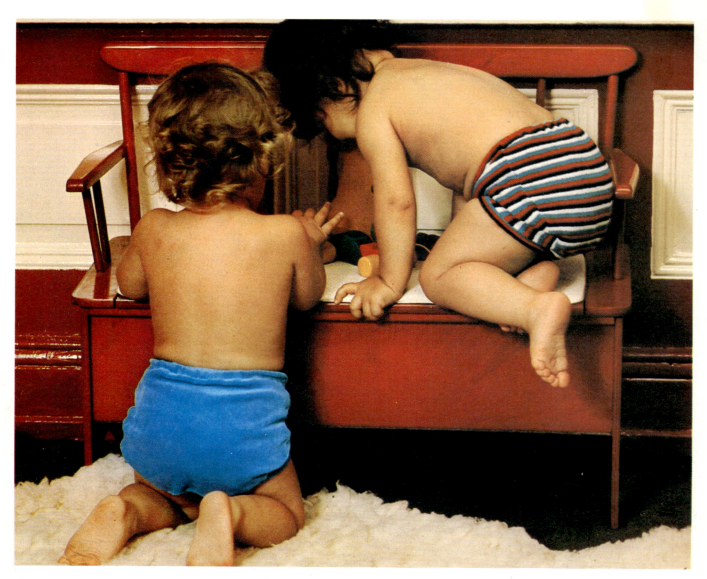

Smartie pants

Size: To fit a child 2–3 years old.

Materials Required: Stretch towelling or velour: 0.30 m ($\frac{3}{8}$ yd), 90 cm (36") wide. Elastic: 0.45 m ($\frac{1}{2}$ yd), 0.5 cm ($\frac{1}{4}$") wide.

Enlarging the pattern: $\frac{1}{4}$ of pants is shown on diagram. Draw the pattern to the measurements.

Cutting out: Seam allowance: Add 2.5 cm (1") at waist, elsewhere 0.5 cm ($\frac{1}{4}$"). Cut out pants back and front in single fabric. Mark the leg slits and the seam on front part. For binding the leg slits, cut 2 straight strips each 21 cm (8$\frac{1}{4}$") long and 3 cm (1$\frac{1}{4}$") wide.

Sewing: Stitch with short zigzag stitches. Bind the leg slits as follows: cut along the marked line from lower edge to upper end of slit. Stitch one edge of strips around slit, right sides facing, beginning and ending 2 cm ($\frac{3}{4}$") from lower edge. Fold strip in half lengthwise, turn in raw edge, and stitch along previous seamline. Finish raw edges together. Stitch the 2 cm ($\frac{3}{4}$") seam beneath the leg slit, together with the end of the strip. This will result in a little loss of width which can be adjusted by stretching. Stitch the 2 pants parts together. Turn under the seam allowance at waist and stitch 1.5 cm ($\frac{5}{8}$") from the edge, leaving a small opening for the elastic. Draw elastic through.

Inch equivalents:

0.5 cm $=\frac{1}{4}$"	3 cm $=1\frac{1}{8}$"	7 cm $=2\frac{3}{4}$"
1.5 cm $=\frac{5}{8}$"	4.5 cm $=1\frac{7}{8}$"	10 cm $=3\frac{7}{8}$"
2 cm $=\frac{3}{4}$"	5 cm $=2$"	10.5 cm $=4\frac{1}{8}$"
2.5 cm $=1$"	6 cm $=2\frac{3}{8}$"	12.5 cm $=5$"

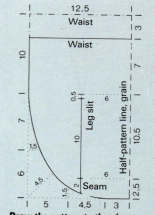

Draw the pattern to the given measurements. Numbers are centimeters; inches are above.

2-year-old: _____
3-year-old: – – – – –

116

Two jolly laundry bags

Mr & Mrs Tidy

3cm	=1¼"
4cm	=1⅝"
6cm	=2½"
10cm	=4"
12cm	=4¾"
13cm	=5¼"
15cm	=6"
16cm	=6⅜"
17cm	=6¾"
20cm	=8"
22cm	=8⅝"
30cm	=12"
45cm	=17¾"
65cm	=25¾"

The photograph below shows the back view. The diagram gives the pattern. Measurements are given in centimeters. Inch equivalents are given above right.

Making the bags

Cut out all pieces twice, adding 1 cm (⅜") seam allowance. Sew pockets onto bag front. Stitch legs together and turn. Stitch front and back together, catching in legs, and turn. Cut a slit 30 cm (11¾") long down the center back and finish the raw edges.

For the face, cut the hair from printed fabric and stitch on. Embroider eyes and mouth, and the hair on the man's face.

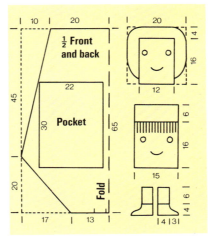

Make a loop for hanging from a 10 cm (4") long bias strip. Stitch the head together, catching in the loop firmly, and leaving neck open. Turn to right side. Fold upper edge of the bag into pleats and baste. Turn under seam allowance on neck edge and place over bag edge. Stitch through all layers. Necktie: Cut a strip 50 cm (19½") x 6 cm (2½"), plus seam allowance. Stitch together and turn. Fasten at neck.

117

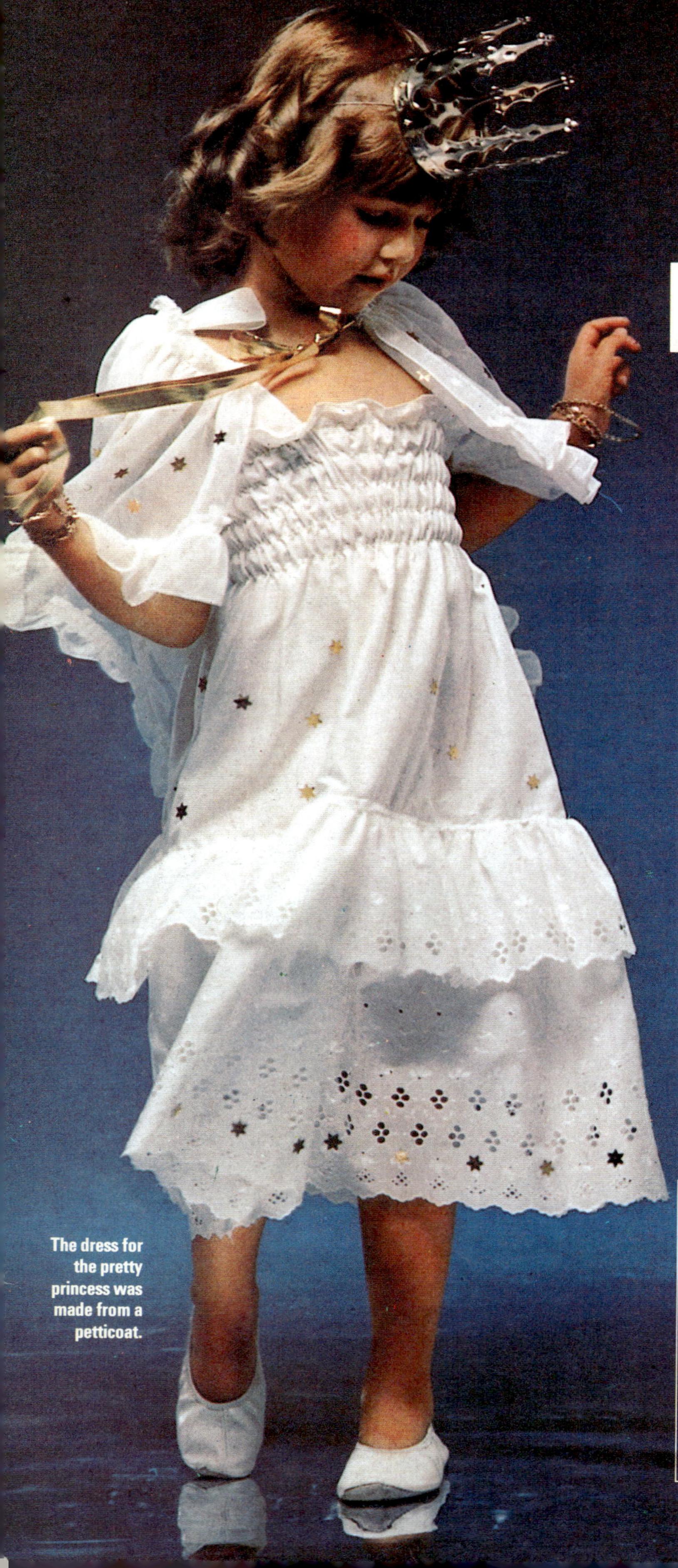

The dress for the pretty princess was made from a petticoat.

Come to the party!

You can make the most inventive costumes for your children by using worn-out garments and remnants of fabric.

Clown costume: This is made from a pair of old pyjama pants. Measure the length, allowing extra for ankle casing, and cut off excess. Over the knees, sew on patches with large stitches; add pockets at the right height. Draw elastic through at the waist and ankles. Make the red straps by gluing felt onto 4 cm ($1\frac{1}{2}''$) wide strips of cotton. The buttons are also covered in felt. Cross the straps over at the back and fasten with a safety pin. Then all that's left to do is to make a large felt bow tie. Iron a firm interfacing onto the felt before cutting out. Cut a strip 10 cm (4″) wide and 25 cm (10″) long, sew the ends together, and wrap a strip 4 cm ($1\frac{1}{2}''$) wide and 12 cm ($4\frac{3}{4}''$) long around the center. Glue yellow dots all over it (you can make these with a punch). Sew a piece of elastic to it for tying it on. The hat and nose can be bought from novelty shops.

Pirate costume: This was created from a pair of old jeans. Sew on patches by hand, cut one leg into fringes and roll up the other one. For the belt, cut a strip of fabric 30 cm ($11\frac{3}{4}''$) wide and 1 m (40″) long. For the headband, cut a strip 12 cm ($4\frac{3}{4}''$) wide and 90 cm (36″) long. The eye patch can be made from black felt. Add a striped T-shirt and a felt bolero cut to the measurements given on the diagram below.

Princess' dress: Use an old petticoat for this costume. If it is too long, shorten it at the top edge and finish the raw edge. With elastic thread on the bobbin, make 5 rows of stitching, each 2.5 cm (1″) apart, and gather to the child's measurements. Add lace trimmings or an embroidered cotton ruffle. For the straps, use 4 ribbons 4 cm ($1\frac{1}{2}''$) wide and 50 cm (20″) long. Tie them into bows on the shoulders. The cape was made from a net curtain. Finish the raw edge and gather to the desired width. Sew on long strips of gold ribbon for ties. For the final touch, stick little golden paper stars onto the skirt and cape.

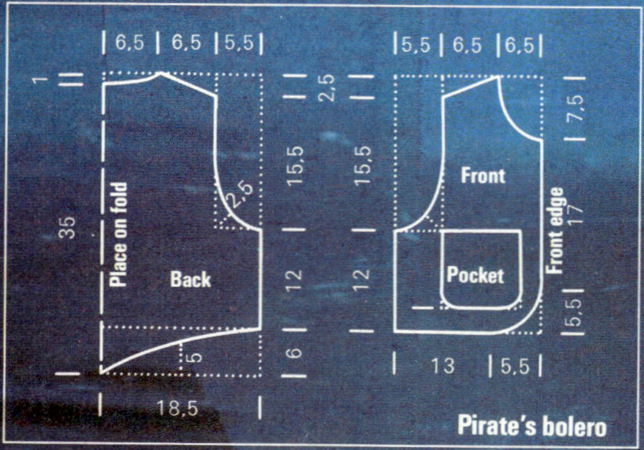

1 cm = $\frac{3}{8}''$
2.5 cm = 1″
5 cm = 2″
5.5 cm = $2\frac{1}{4}''$
6 cm = $2\frac{3}{8}''$
6.5 cm = $2\frac{5}{8}''$
7.5 cm = $2\frac{7}{8}''$
12 cm = $4\frac{3}{4}''$
13 cm = $5\frac{1}{4}''$
15.5 cm = 6″
17 cm = $6\frac{5}{8}''$
18.5 cm = $7\frac{1}{2}''$
35 cm = $13\frac{3}{4}''$

The clown looks very jolly in his baggy pants and zany bow tie.

A pair of old jeans and a few remnants transformed him into a pirate.

Playing Indians
is always a favorite
game, so make these
colorful costumes
for your tribe.

Fringed and feathered

Size: 6–8 year olds, height 116 cm – 128 cm ($45\frac{1}{2}''$ – $50\frac{1}{2}''$). Check lengths first and make any adjustments necessary before cutting out the pattern pieces.

GIRL'S TUNIC

Materials Required: Light brown felt: 0.60 m ($\frac{5}{8}$ yd), 180 cm (72") wide. Dark brown felt: 0.10 m ($\frac{1}{8}$ yd), 180 cm (72") wide. Felt pieces in yellow, red, orange, blue. 1 button. Fabric glue.

Cutting out: Cut out the pieces with 1 cm ($\frac{3}{8}''$) seam allowance, but no allowance at the hem. Fringe: With pinking shears, cut 2 dark brown strips 26 cm x 7 cm ($10\frac{1}{4}''$ x $2\frac{3}{4}''$). Cut fringe to a depth of 5.5 cm ($2\frac{1}{4}''$). Felt strips: Cut these 1 cm ($\frac{3}{8}''$) wide with pinking shears.

Sewing: Glue felt strips to the front neck and sleeves 1 cm ($\frac{3}{8}''$) apart. Join the seams, catching in the fringe on the inner sleeve seams. Turn in the seam allowance at the neck and sleeve hem and stitch. Glue felt strips at the hem. Sew on the button and a loop.

HEAD DRESS

Materials Required: Light brown felt: 0.10 m ($\frac{1}{8}$ yd), 180 cm (72") wide. Heavy non-woven interfacing: 0.10 m ($\frac{1}{8}$ yd), 82 cm (32") wide. Narrow braid: 1.25 m ($1\frac{3}{8}$ yds) each in yellow, red, and blue. Feather. Velcro: 10 cm (4").

Cutting out: Cut 1 strip each of felt and interfacing 55 cm x 9 cm ($21\frac{5}{8}''$ x $3\frac{1}{2}''$).

Sewing: Fold the interfacing in half lengthwise. Baste on the felt and stitch on the braid. Stitch on the Velcro to close the ends.

SANDALS

Materials Required: Felt: 0.10 m ($\frac{1}{8}$ yd), 180 cm (72") wide. Rubber sandals. Fabric glue.

Cutting out: With pinking shears, cut 4 strips 110 cm ($43\frac{1}{2}''$) long, 2 strips 15 cm (6") long, and 2 strips 50 cm ($19\frac{1}{2}''$) long, all 1 cm ($\frac{3}{8}''$) wide.

Glue onto sandals as in the photograph.

BOY'S TUNIC

Materials Required: Light brown felt: 0.60 m ($\frac{5}{8}$ yd), 180 cm (72") wide. Yellow felt: 0.10 m ($\frac{1}{8}$ yd), 180 cm (72") wide. Narrow braid: 4.20 m ($4\frac{5}{8}$ yds) each of yellow, blue, and red. 1 button.

Cutting out: There is no seam allowance at neck and hem, elsewhere 1 cm ($\frac{3}{8}''$). Fringe: With pinking shears, cut 4 strips of each of following lengths: 24 cm, 44 cm, and 29 cm ($9\frac{1}{2}''$, $17\frac{3}{4}''$, and $11\frac{3}{8}''$) by 5 cm (2") wide. Cut fringe to a depth of 4 cm ($1\frac{1}{2}''$). Cut 1 yellow strip 34 cm ($13\frac{1}{2}''$) long and 1 cm ($\frac{3}{8}''$) wide with pinking shears for the neck edge.

Sewing: Stitch braids 0.3 cm ($\frac{1}{8}''$) apart and stitch the fringes on below. Join the seams and press open. Stitch on the felt strip at the neck. Turn under and stitch the sleeve hem. Sew on the button and a loop.

PANTS

Materials Required: Light brown felt: 0.55 m ($\frac{5}{8}$ yd), 180 cm (72") wide. Dark brown felt: 0.10 m ($\frac{1}{8}$ yd), 180 cm (72") wide. Felt pieces in red, orange, yellow. Elastic. Fabric glue.

Cutting out: Cut out twice with a 1 cm ($\frac{3}{8}''$) seam allowance all around. With pinking shears, cut felt strips 45 cm ($17\frac{3}{4}''$) long by 1 cm ($\frac{3}{8}''$) wide. Fringe: With pinking shears, cut 2 strips 62 cm ($24\frac{3}{8}''$) long, 7 cm ($2\frac{3}{4}''$) wide. Cut fringe to a depth of 5 cm (2").

Sewing: Glue on strips at the hem. Join inside leg seam, then crotch seam. Turn in waist seam and draw through elastic. Stitch on the fringe along line marked on pattern.

HEAD DRESS

Materials Required: Felt: 0.10 m ($\frac{1}{8}$ yd), 180 cm (72") wide. Felt pieces in yellow, red, orange. Heavy non-woven interfacing: 0.10 m ($\frac{1}{8}$ yd), 82 cm (32") wide. 13 feathers. Velcro: 10 cm (4").

Cutting out: Cut 1 felt, 1 interfacing strip 55 cm x 9 cm ($21\frac{1}{2}''$ x $3\frac{1}{2}''$). Cut felt strips 1 cm ($\frac{3}{8}''$) wide.

Sewing: Fold interfacing in half lengthwise, baste the felt around it and sew on the feathers 4 cm ($1\frac{1}{2}''$) apart. Stitch on the felt strips. At the ends, stitch on Velcro.

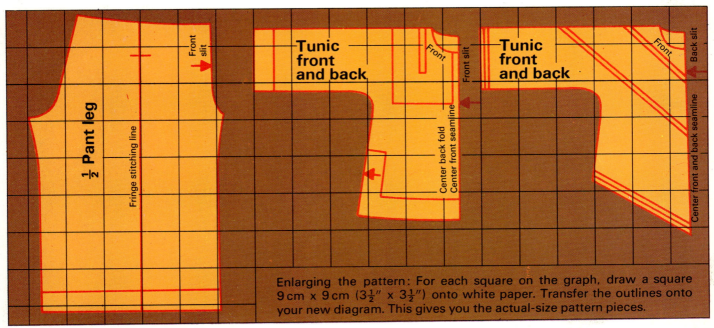

Enlarging the pattern: For each square on the graph, draw a square 9 cm x 9 cm ($3\frac{1}{2}''$ x $3\frac{1}{2}''$) onto white paper. Transfer the outlines onto your new diagram. This gives you the actual-size pattern pieces.

So easy to make

For young swingers

Here's a hammock specially designed for younger children. It's perfect for those long summer days and rolls up compactly to take on picnics. Made of heavy, unbleached cotton it's tough enough to withstand any amount of swinging, and is very quick and simple to construct.

Here you can see one of the long sides of the hammock. A length of cord is drawn through a casing and the fabric is gathered up along it.

The wooden strips at each short side have a notch cut into each end. The rope is fastened so that it rests in the notch and cannot slip out.

The wooden strip is pushed through a wide casing at each end of the hammock and the fabric is gathered up to expose the notches at either end.

It is very important to fix the rope for hanging securely to a tree or hook. Make a suitably strong knot which cannot slip or work undone.

Materials Required:

Be sure you use strong materials which will stand up to a lot of wear and tear. Heavy unbleached cotton: 3.10 m (3⅜ yds), 90 cm (36") wide. 2 wooden strips: 60 cm (23¾") long, 5 cm (2") wide, and 2 cm (¾") thick. Thick cord: 1.60 m (1¾ yds). Strong rope, such as a washing line. (Use plenty of rope to enable you to hang the hammock on higher or wider-spaced trees if necessary.)

Making the hammock

Cut the 3.10 m (3½ yds) length of fabric widthwise into 2 pieces [i.e., each piece measures 1.55 m (1¾ yds)]. With right sides facing, stitch the 2 pieces together along both long edges, close to the selvages. Turn to the right side, then make a 1.5 cm (⅝") hem along each long side, thus forming a casing for the cord. Cut the cord in half and pull through the casing on each side. Gather up the fabric to measure 76 cm (30") and pin firmly to the cord to hold the ends in place.
On the short sides, make casings for the wooden strips. Turn under raw edges 1 cm (⅜"), then 10 cm (4"). Stitch down twice, catching in the ends of the cord. (If the cord is too thick for the sewing machine, sew it securely by hand).
Make a notch at each end of the wooden strips, 3 cm (1¼") away from the edge. Push the strips through the 2 wide casings and gather up the fabric until the notches are exposed.
Knot a length of rope into each notch so that it cannot slip out. Then at each end of the hammock, knot the lengths of rope together at a point equidistant from the notches (see large photograph). The hammock is now ready to hang.

Easy riders

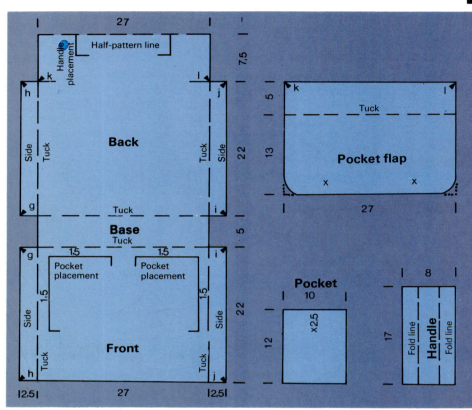

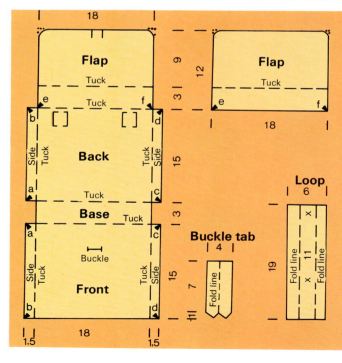

Enlarge the pattern pieces to the measurements given. Numbers are centimeters. Inches are given below.

1 cm	$=\frac{3}{8}''$
1.5 cm	$=\frac{5}{8}''$
2.5 cm	$=1''$
3 cm	$=1\frac{1}{4}''$
4 cm	$=1\frac{5}{8}''$
5 cm	$=2''$
6 cm	$=2\frac{3}{8}''$
7 cm	$=2\frac{3}{4}''$
7.5 cm	$=2\frac{7}{8}''$
8 cm	$=3\frac{1}{8}''$
9 cm	$=3\frac{1}{2}''$
10 cm	$=4''$
12 cm	$=4\frac{3}{4}''$
13 cm	$=5\frac{1}{4}''$
15 cm	$=6''$
17 cm	$=6\frac{3}{4}''$
18 cm	$=7\frac{1}{8}''$
19 cm	$=7\frac{1}{2}''$
22 cm	$=8\frac{5}{8}''$
27 cm	$=10\frac{5}{8}''$

Trying to cycle with a bag dangling precariously from the handlebars or jammed onto the carrier is annoying and can be dangerous if it gets in the way. So make sure the children carry their belongings safely packed away in these ingenious bicycle bags.

Blue saddle bag

Materials Required: Blue sailcloth: 0.70 m ($\frac{3}{4}$ yd), 120 cm (48″) wide. White sailcloth: 0.15 m ($\frac{1}{8}$ yd), 120 cm (48″) wide. 4 press studs or snaps. Leather needle.

Cutting out: Half of the bag pattern is shown on the blue diagram. Enlarge all pieces to the measurements given. The distance between points **l** and **k** may be adjusted, depending on the width of your luggage rack. Cut out the bag, adding 3 cm (1$\frac{1}{4}$″) at the top edge of the fronts and 1 cm ($\frac{3}{8}$″) on all other edges. Cut out the pocket flap 4 times with 0.5 cm ($\frac{1}{4}$″) seam allowance. Cut out the patch pockets 4 times with a 3 cm (1$\frac{1}{4}$″) seam allowance at the upper edge, otherwise 1 cm ($\frac{3}{8}$″). Cut handle to measurements given.

Sewing: Press the seam allowance of the patch pockets to the inside and stitch them on where marked. Finish all cut edges of the bag except for the side seams. Fold in the seam allowance at the top edge of the fronts, snip diagonally into the corners, and stitch down. Along the center of the bag bases, stitch a 0.2 cm ($\frac{1}{16}$″) wide pin tuck from the wrong side. Join the side seams, and cutting away any excess fabric, finish the edges together. Join the sides to the base of the bag. Now stitch pin tucks along the marked lines from the right side. Turn under the raw edges along the center section of the bag and top-stitch. Stitch 2 sets of flaps together, snip diagonally across corners, turn, and top-stitch. Finish the edges together along the straight edge. Make a pin tuck along the marked line from the outside and stitch the flap to the bag, right sides facing and matching points **k** and **l**. Handle: turn in 0.5 cm ($\frac{1}{4}$") seam allowance and fold the strip twice lengthwise so that the edges meet at the center of the underside. Stitch along the handle several times and stitch to the bag where marked. Finally, punch in press studs or snaps where indicated.

Yellow handlebar bag
Materials Required: Sailcloth: 0.30 m ($\frac{3}{8}$ yd), 120 cm (48") wide. 1 buckle without prong. Piece of stiff, transparent plastic for name plate. 2 press studs or snaps. Leather needle.

Cutting out: The whole bag pattern is shown on the yellow diagram. Enlarge it to the measurements given. Cut out the bag with a 1 cm ($\frac{3}{8}$") seam allowance all around, except for the flap which has 0.5 cm ($\frac{1}{4}$"). Cut loops and buckle tab to measurements given.

Sewing: Finish the front top edge and side edges of the base. Stitch the bag flap sections together, snip diagonally across corners, turn, and top-stitch. Stitch the piece of plastic for the name plate onto the flap as shown. Turn in the seam allowance along the front top edge and stitch. Stitch a 0.2 cm ($\frac{1}{16}$") wide pin tuck along the base of the bag from the inside. Join the side seams and, cutting off any excess fabric, finish the edges together. Join the sides to the bag base. Stitch pin tucks along the marked lines from the right side. At the tuck of the self flap, catch in and cut edge of the stitched-on flap. Buckle tab: turn in 0.5 cm ($\frac{1}{4}$") on the long edges and at the point. Fold in half and stitch together close to the edge. Finish the straight edge and stitch to the flap along the top-stitching line. Loops: turn in 0.5 cm ($\frac{1}{4}$") on the narrow sides, then on long sides. Turn under along the fold lines so that the edges meet at the center. Top-stitch. Punch in the press studs or snaps and stitch the loops to the bag with a decorative cross. Finally, sew on the buckle.

The smaller bag loops over the handlebars and can also be worn with a belt. The loops can also be snapped together to form a handle. ▶

This bag fits snugly over the carrier. Pick it up and it becomes a satchel.

Made of sailcloth

All packed up for school

A satchel with a place for everything so that nothing will ever get lost again! It's cheap to make and light to carry.

Materials Required: Piece of sailcloth: 50 cm x 100 cm ($19\frac{5}{8}''$ x $39\frac{3}{8}''$). Carpet tape: 1.40 m ($1\frac{5}{8}$yds), 3 cm ($1\frac{1}{4}''$) wide. Buckle: 3 cm ($1\frac{1}{4}''$) wide. 4 eyelets. 1 press stud or snap.

Making the satchel

Cut out the whole bag twice, following the measurements on the diagram and adding 1 cm ($\frac{3}{8}''$) seam allowance. Stitch together, right sides facing, and turn. Cut out the pocket once, with 1 cm ($\frac{3}{8}''$) seam allowance at the sides and 2 cm ($\frac{3}{4}''$) at the top edge. Press under the seam allowances.

Cut out the space for the label, turn back the raw edges and top-stitch. Then top-stitch the pocket to the bag front 3 cm ($1\frac{1}{4}''$) from the top edge. Make 4 vertical rows and 1 horizontal row of stitching as shown on the diagram.

Cut the carpet tape into 2 lengths of 90 cm ($35\frac{1}{2}''$) and 50 cm ($19\frac{1}{2}''$). Sew the buckle to the shorter length. Trim one end of the longer piece to a point and finish the raw edges. Punch in the eyelets on the long piece about 4 cm ($1\frac{1}{2}''$) apart. Stitch the other 2 ends of the tapes to the wrong side of the bag base. Then pin the edges of the tapes to the front and back side edges, wrong sides facing.

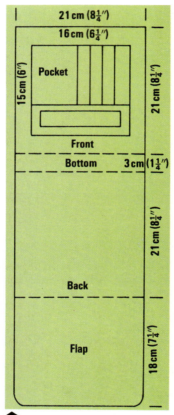

Cut out the fabric according to the measurements given on the diagram.

Diagram labels:
- 21 cm ($8\frac{1}{4}''$)
- 16 cm ($6\frac{1}{4}''$)
- 15 cm (6") — Pocket
- 21 cm ($8\frac{1}{4}''$)
- Front
- Bottom — 3 cm ($1\frac{1}{4}''$)
- 21 cm ($8\frac{1}{4}''$)
- Back
- Flap — 18 cm ($7\frac{1}{4}''$)

Made of sailcloth, the satchel is very tough. Carpet tape is stitched around the base and sides to form the gusset and strap. ▶

Stitch together, close to the tape edges. Top-stitch the flap and bag top the same distance from the edge. Punch a press stud into the flap and front.

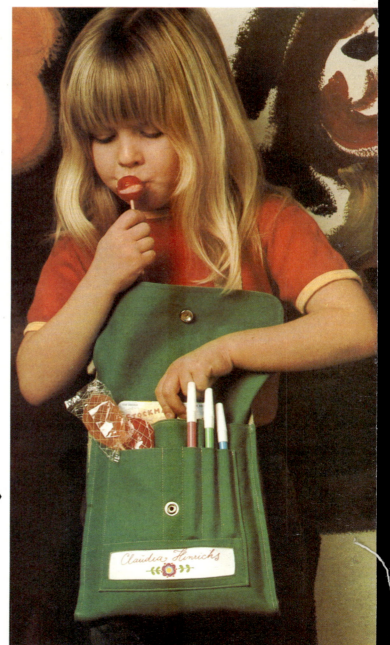

INDEX

INDEX